Understanding the Brahma Kumaris

Understanding the Brahma Kumaris

Frank Whaling
Professor Emeritus, The Study of Religion
University of Edinburgh

Third Eye
BOOKS FOR YOUR WELL BEING

Understanding the Brahma Kumaris / ***Frank Whaling***

First Indian Edition 2013

ISBN 978-81-8274-730-2

First published by Dunedin Academic Press Ltd, Hudson House, 8 Albany Street, Edinburgh EH1 3QB. This edition published in arrangement

Published in India by
THIRD EYE
Imprint of
PENTAGON PRESS
206, Peacock Lane, Shahpur Jat
New Delhi-110049
Phones: 011-64706243, 26491568
Telefax: 011-26490600
email: rajan@pentagonpress.in
website: www.pentagonpress.in

Printed at Aegean Offset Printers, Greater Noida

Dedication

For a number of Brahma Kumaris,
especially Sister Jayanti, Sister Louisa and Sister Maureen,
who have given significant help in the wrting of this book

Contents

List of Illustrations

Introduction

It has been my privilege to be the general editor of the series entitled *Understanding Faith* to which this book belongs. The series has covered the three main monotheistic religions — the Christian, Muslim and Jewish traditions — as well as three religions that arose in India — the Hindu, Buddhist and Sikh traditions. The Baha'i tradition that started in the Middle East in the nineteenth century has also been discussed. The series concludes by engaging with two further traditions — Chinese religions and the Brahma Kumaris.

The Brahma Kumaris are the newest of all these traditions. Indeed this movement began (at roughly the same time as the writer was born) in the twentieth century and has developed and spread during the lifetime of most readers of this book. The Brahma Kumari tradition, as with all spiritual traditions, is different, bewildering and fascinating in its complexity, and its newness adds to its attraction. I have found it rewarding and insightful to engage with the Brahma Kumaris, who have been generous with their help.

It is one thing to describe the Brahma Kumaris. It is another to understand them. The aim of this work is to try to do both. I will therefore mainly use phenomenology. First, this involves putting one's own world-view aside in order to understand the world-view of others and to see them 'as they are', unhindered by one's own prejudices. The technical term for this is epoche, and the aim is to avoid bias. The second element in phenomenology is empathy. This has the positive aim of engaging sympathetically with the world-view of others in order to try and see them as they see themselves. It is to try to understand, as far as is possible, from within. If the readers are not Brahma Kumaris they can attempt to empathise with those who are, and if they are Brahma Kumaris they may gain new insights into their own community.

It is difficult however for 'outsiders' to become 'insiders'. I am a white male who was born in Yorkshire (in England, in Europe) but now lives in Scotland; I am also a professor and a Christian. It is not easy to put all that background and environment on one side. Total empathy and total objectivity, although they may be desirable, are virtually impossible to achieve. We are all laden with inherent baggage.

Fortunately, it is possible to exercise a kind of self-reflexive phenomenology. The process can be ongoing and cumulative. By entering more deeply into another tradition through study, research, travel and deep conversations about findings and observations, one is better able and better equipped to understand others. Therefore having talked to and engaged with the Brahma Kumaris about their own 'faithful intentions', I feel better able to understand what their life is all about.

After a very brief history of the rise and growth of the Brahma Kumari tradition in this introduction, I will recount four vignettes, four personal stories, about the Brahma Kumaris in order to introduce the adherents themselves and provide a basic and immediate sense of what they are about. In the rest of the book I will go into more detail about their history, and I will also use elements from my own model of religion to bring out the view of transcendence in the tradition and the mediating focus whereby this becomes known. In the later stages of *Understanding the Brahma Kumaris* I will engage in a deeper analysis of eight elements within the Brahma Kumari tradition. These will focus on the community itself and its inward life; on the regular practices of the community; on the ethical convictions lying behind its work; on the social involvement of the Brahma Kumaris in wider society; on their concepts; on their aesthetics; on their spirituality, which is, I will suggest, the most important element in their life; and on their **murlis** (a message for each day, akin to a kind of scripture). After analysing the crucial elements of their faith, the book ends with a brief estimate of where the Brahma Kumaris are now, and of what may lie ahead for the movement.

A Very Brief History of the Brahma Kumaris

The Brahma Kumaris started in 1936 in the city of Hyderabad in the Sind province of India. Hyderabad was then in British India (it is now in Pakistan). At around the age of sixty a benign millionaire diamond merchant named Lekhraj Khubchand began to have visions. These were so exceptional that they caused him to sell his share in a successful diamond business and start a series of meetings in his home, which were attended mainly by women. This was the beginning of the new movement — a female member being known as a Brahma Kumari and a man as a Brahma Kumar. Dada Lekhraj, as he became affectionately known, used his fortune to set up a trust led by eleven young women. One of the young women, later known as Om Radhe, became the leader of the new movement, while Dada Lekhraj remained the key figure in the whole enterprise.

The exceptional nature of the Brahma Kumaris' life and work, particularly the stress on the pivotal role of women in this new movement, led to local persecution, and a move from Hyderabad to Karachi. There the Brahma Kumaris were able to live quietly during the Second World War, taking stock of their situation and preparing for their future work. Following the partition of British India in 1947 the Brahma Kumaris felt that it was time to move again — this time to Mount Abu in Rajasthan in India, and this remains their headquarters today. From Mount Abu the Brahma Kumaris could visit family and friends who had also moved to India, and so Brahma Kumari centres were established in Delhi, Lucknow, Kolkata (Calcutta), Mumbai (Bombay), Amritsar and Bangalore.

In 1954 the Brahma Kumaris made their first venture outside India — they sent a delegation under the guidance of Dadi Prakashmani to the 1954 World Religious Congress in Japan. On their homeward voyage the Brahma Kumari delegates visited Hong Kong, Singapore, Indonesia and Malaysia. However as yet, no lasting outreach work was established.

After the death of Om Radhe in 1965, Dadi Prakashmani succeeded Om Radhe as administrative head of the movement. On 18 January 1969 Dada Lekhraj, who had become known as Brahma Baba, passed away. The day of his death became a day of remembrance for Brahma Kumaris around the world, and a memorial was set up for him on Mount Abu.

It might have been expected that the deaths of these two key Brahma Kumari figures — Om Radhe and Brahma Baba — would cause a decline in the movement, the deaths of founder figures usually triggering times of crisis in religious history. However just the opposite occurred. From that period significant outreach work began outside India as well as in India. A key overseas centre was set up in London in the early 1970s and it was led by a gifted Brahma Kumari named Dadi Janki (illus. 0.1) Over the next twenty years, 212 centres and eighty sub-centres were founded in seventy countries around the world. This expansion was spearheaded partly from the London centre. Eventually, six zones under regional co-ordinating offices were established: the international headquarters along with India came under Mount Abu; Russia and the Baltic states, under Moscow; Africa, under Nairobi; North, South, Central America and the Caribbean, under New York; Asia and Australasia, under Sydney; and Europe and the Middle East, under London. In addition, by 1982 there were 850 centres in India.

Between 1980 and 1982 a special Ten-Point Programme for World Welfare was drawn up, and this signalled a desire for the Brahma Kumaris to be more involved in global events. In 1983 their first Universal Peace Conference was held at Mount Abu, and it was followed annually by others. In 1984 Dadi Prakashmani was awarded a United Nations Peace Medal. International conferences were soon held in seven countries. By then Mount Abu

Dadi Janki (right) and Dadi Gulzar, current joint leaders of the Brahma Kumaris.

had a great hall that could seat 3,000 people, and had quarters to accommodate a great number of visitors. By 1987, at the time of its Golden Jubilee, the Brahma Kumaris had evolved dramatically from a small Indian community to a body that could co-ordinate major international projects. These included the 1986 Million Minutes for Peace, which reached eighty-eight countries, and Global Co-operation for a Better World, which was launched from the House of Lords in London in 1988. Other projects included the building of an ultra-modern hospital on Mount Abu to give substantial medical help to the poor villagers on that Indian mountain.

By 2011 there were more than 8,500 Brahma Kumari centres in more than a hundred countries in contact with more than 850,000 students around the world.

Four Vignettes of the Brahma Kumaris

The Brahma Kumaris are a recent movement about which relatively little is known in the academic world or by the wider public so here are four vignettes to demonstrate aspects of the life and work of their adherents.

The first is a description of the staple daily Brahma Kumaris event — the 6.30am gathering. Although the vignette is depicted in Edinburgh,

Scotland, it is typical of what happens in more than 8,500 centres around the world. The second vignette details the launching of the 1993 Year of Inter-Religious Understanding and Co-operation at Global Co-operation House in London, which is the international centre of the Brahma Kumaris World Spiritual University. The third vignette describes the opening of a fine country house at Nuneham Park in Oxfordshire as a global retreat centre run by the Brahma Kumaris on behalf of those who wish to attend retreats there. And finally there is a short sketch of my visit to the world headquarters of the Brahma Kumaris on Mount Abu in India.

An Early Morning Gathering in Edinburgh

It is after 6am on a damp Edinburgh winter's morning. About fifteen people arrive — on foot, by bicycle, in cars — at a house situated in the middle of a typical Edinburgh sandstone apartment block. They enter, remove their shoes and go along a short corridor that leads off into a room on the left. They sit down on the floor in a position appropriate for meditation. Chairs are brought to the room for those who are elderly or infirm. All those present look towards a woman in white, who is seated facing them. Also at the front is a large photograph of an elderly silver-haired Indian gentleman with a pleasant smile. Soft music is played on a tape recorder as the Brahma Kumaris meditate. From time to time the woman at the front looks in turn at each of the people present, and they return her gaze.

At about 6.30am the young man in charge of the tape recorder turns it off. There is a short period of silent meditation. Then the white-clothed lady begins to read the murli (a message) to the assembled company. This takes about thirty-five minutes. After the murli has finished there is another short period of meditation, a period of conversation about the murli, and some notices are given concerning the community. At about 8am the Brahma Kumaris disperse to go about their daily work.

This same sequence of activities happens every day in every centre around the world ranging from Delhi to Russia, from Austria to Dubai, from Botswana to Surinam, and from Australia to the United States. The daily murli is sent from India and then translated into local languages. Using a special website it is possible for translations to be made in advance so that now, on every day of the week, at roughly 6.30am, the same murli is being read at the same time in thousands of centres around the world.

Who then are these people? Why is a woman their leader? Who is the silver-haired gentleman in the large photograph? Why do they meditate at 6.30 every morning? What is it all about?

The Launch of the 1993 Year of Inter-Religious Understanding and Co-operation

Nearly 600 people gather on the morning of 27 January 1993 at Global Co-operation House in London. The Brahma Kumaris offered to host this assembly, and those present belong to different religious traditions. They are here by invitation to celebrate the centenary of the 1893 World Parliament of Religion (held in Chicago) and to inaugurate 1993 as a Year of Inter-Religious Understanding and Co-operation.

There is an air of expectancy as leading actors, such as Jane Lapotaire, Clarke Peters and Robin Ramsay, read extracts from the account of the 1893 Parliament that are both informative and amusing. Its atmosphere is skilfully recreated; its uniqueness is evoked. There is laughter as great cheers greet the conservative Christian preacher Cook as he promises that salvation is only through Christ, and equally great cheers greet Swami Vivekananda, the influential Hindu, as he talks about the transcendental unity of all religions. By the time these readings are finished, the hall is full.

Dadi Janki, a co-leader of the Brahma Kumaris, welcomes everyone — her Hindi address being translated into English. Her powerful use of silent meditation then sets the atmosphere for this inter-faith assembly a hundred years after the Chicago gathering.

For the rest of the morning there is a fascinating succession of speeches and events. Five keynote addresses are given by: the Most Reverend Trevor Huddleston, president of the Anti-Apartheid Movement; Dr Mai Yamani, a female Muslim social anthropologist from Oxford University; Swami Bhavyananda, president of the Ramakrishna Vedanta Centre; Rabbi Hugo Gryn, the Jewish Co-ordinator of the Inter-Faith Network; and Dr Edgar Mitchell, one of the first men to land on the moon, who describes how the experience has changed his life. Interspersed among the addresses are prayers from colourfully dressed representatives of the Baha'i, Buddhist, Christian, Hindu, Jain, Jewish, Muslim, Sikh and Zoroastrian traditions. When they have shared their prayer they stay at the front of the Hall while a companion pours water from a source sacred to that tradition into a fountain specially erected on the platform. Thus water from the Jordan, the Ganges and other sacred rivers mingles. Eventually eighteen people are assembled on the platform in their traditional costumes.

Later on, there are squeals of hilarity as a number of ten-year-old children from a local school rush forward on to the stage to perform a short drama called *Healing the World*. On a stretcher they bear a deflated-looking world, which gradually revives because of the efforts of these youngsters from different races, who end up singing Michael Jackson's 'Heal the World'. As they do so, the screen on the stage rises up to reveal a 'One World Quilt of Unity' from Milton Keynes. It contains seventy colourful patchwork pieces produced by two hundred people from Milton Keynes with diverse faith and cultural backgrounds.

In the afternoon everyone takes part in six lively workshops on the themes of peace, love, respect, humility, honesty and justice. Under the chairmanship of a Roman Catholic nun from London who has taken an Indian name, I speak at the workshop on respect, together with the abbot of a Buddhist monastery in Northumberland. Other speakers include the Reverend Kathleen Richardson (the first woman president of the British Methodist Church) and Daniel Gomez-Ibanez from Chicago, whose presence symbolises the centenary of the 1893 Chicago World Parliament of Religions.

The evening is given over to celebration. Children from the Forest School, the Pestalozzi Children's Village and the Jain and Sikh communities lead the celebrations. Later such diverse talents as John Cleese, Hayley Mills, the Reverend Dr Edward Carpenter, Dadi Janki and Edgar Mitchell display their skills. It is an impressive start to an important and historic year.

But who are these Brahma Kumaris that they can organise such a unique event in such an auspicious building, as well as draw together people from all religious traditions when they are relatively unknown themselves? Who is this venerable and spiritual woman Dadi Janki? What is the nature of the Brahma Kumaris' concern for the world and for humanity?

Opening of the Brahma Kumari Global Retreat Centre at Nuneham Park

The setting is Nuneham Park, an elegant eighteenth-century country house in Oxfordshire, with gardens landscaped by Capability Brown which slope down to the quiet waters of the River Thames. Visitors, on Saturday 26 June 1993, are invited to arrive at any time after 3pm to enjoy the beautifully renovated house and gardens, and to take tea served by the community on the lawns in front of the house. At every corner of the house and grounds, guests are greeted by smiling hostesses and hosts answering questions, meeting needs and guiding to the next activity. At 5pm white-robed Brahma Kumaris from centres all over the world, with others in their national and faith costumes, along with their guests, are summoned into a large marquee, at the front of which is a stage decorated with many floral garlands. At the back a group of artists is working on three large canvasses of Nuneham Park House and Gardens. These artists and their activity show that 'when people are happy, they are creative'.

The ceremony is launched with a procession of mummers, morris dancers, musicians and a general sense of carnival, and each event is punctuated by some forms of music, song and dance that illustrate the point that is being made. The different parts of the ceremony are introduced by two compères who begin with the interesting phrase 'dear sisters and aunties'. This gently reminds the audience that they are guests of a movement led by women.

The more formal part of the proceedings starts with a brief appreciation of the beautiful surroundings, and a history of the house. Various speakers, such as Prebendary Marcus Braybrooke and Lord Ennals, communicate their good wishes for the well-being and success of this global retreat centre being opened in the heart of the Oxfordshire countryside.

Three senior Brahma Kumaris have travelled from London, the United States and India to talk about the ideals and visions lying behind their World Spiritual University — a 'university' because, as one speaker says, two bases of their work are knowledge and understanding. The particular points that are emphasised to the guests include peace; the importance of righting the world by starting with one's self; and the need to have confidence that each individual has the spiritual potential to do this. The raja yoga that the community uses in some of its teaching emphasises the 'royal dignity' of each soul, and this is brought out in the gentle meditation that forms the ending of the formal proceedings. Before the mummers, morris dancers and musicians take the marquee guests back outside, there is a reading of a famous passage about the spiritual journey from T. S. Eliot's 'Little Gidding':

> We shall not cease from exploration
> And the end of all our exploring
> Will be to arrive where we started
> And know it for the first time (Eliot, 1944).

Guests and community then spill out on to the lawns for a vegetarian supper, and to continue the meetings and conversations begun earlier in the day. For this event the community has combined things English with things Indian — a memorable exercise in the transplantation of religious life.

Again the question is raised: what is this community that crosses over national and religious boundaries, wears white clothes, practises raja yoga and is able to open such a splendid retreat centre in the heart of Oxfordshire?

Arriving at the Headquarters of the Brahma Kumaris

In 1987 my plane arrives at Delhi airport, one of the two main entry points to India for overseas visitors to Madhuban, the headquarters of the Brahma

Kumaris on Mount Abu in Rajasthan. After a brief visit to one of the Brahma Kumari centres in Delhi and a pleasant but short meeting with the leader of the centre, Dadi Gulzar, who is the trance medium of the movement, and with Jagdish Chander, who is the main writer of the movement, it is time to board the night train for Abu Road. The first-class sleeper is well appointed. The station sights and sounds are typically Indian — the cries advertising food and hot tea, the drifting smoke from biri cigarettes, the swaying mass of bodies and the sounds of engines manoeuvring. Finally the train sets off on its 465-mile journey to Abu Road, the railway station built in the days of the British Raj as the connecting point to the hill resort of Mount Abu.

A car sent by the Brahma Kumaris is there to greet me and I am driven up the mountain. It is early November and the weather has been warm on the arid plains of Rajasthan, which the train has passed through. As the car winds sixteen miles up the mountain road, it becomes noticeably cooler. The British knew what they were doing when they retreated here from the burning heat of the Indian summer, and the Brahma Kumaris have maintained their nerve-centre here on this scenic plateau set within the range of the Aravali hills.

As the upper layers of the serpentine road are reached, pine trees and silver birches are visible. In flowering shrubs and bushes birds are singing, an occasional peacock is seen and a startled animal scuttles across the road. This is a place of beauty, and this impression is confirmed as the top is reached and a delightful lake comes into view. Its name is Nakhi Lake because such loveliness could only have been dug out by the ***nakh*** (nails) of the gods. Boats skim across the waters, skirting small islands, and its shores are covered by magnificent lawns and beds of flowers. This splendour and solitude, the driver explains, has attracted religious aspirants down the ages, including the Jains, who in the eleventh and twelfth centuries built the exquisite Dilwara Temple on Mount Abu; and the great Vaishnava Hindu leader Ramananda, who in the fourteenth century installed a famous image in the elegant Raghunath temple by the lake; while the founder of the modern Hindu Arya Samaj, Swami Dayananda, meditated here between 1852 and 1854.

But where is Madhuban, the 'Forest of Honey', the Brahma Kumari headquarters? It does not come into view immediately. A first impression of Mount Abu is of a jumble of shops, eating places, craft centres, and all the benign chaos that is apparent in many Indian towns. And then a different kind of edifice comes into view. It is a building, indeed a cluster of buildings, of sleek whiteness that stands out in the bespattered greyness that elsewhere betokens the depredations of the monsoon. It is Madhuban. It seems strikingly different, almost too different, from its surroundings.

Neatness, whiteness and beauty are the words that sum up my first sense of Madhuban. There is a sensation of smiles and welcomes, a number of pleasant introductions, and a helping hand to my abode for the next three weeks. My dormitory is a small one containing a number of beds for men, and I make myself at home for I will be the only one staying in it during this period. It is a quiet time for entertaining Western visitors. I am able to be here in November because it is part of my sabbatical leave from Edinburgh University. A number of Indian visitors are attending courses but they have their own quarters. A short distance away a gang of workmen are erecting a huge building that will house many more visitors under one roof. The sound of their efforts will continue into the night as they work towards the deadline of an imminent conference.

After an appetising lunch and a short rest it is time to be shown around Madhuban. In the entrance hall to the great auditorium, there are seven large paintings, which depict the original visions of the founder of the movement, Dada Lekhraj. He is the person whose photograph had been present in the centre in Edinburgh. The paintings show, in order, a vision of the Hindu deity **Vishnu** by means of which Dada Lekhraj knew that he had been called to be a revealer of God; a vision of a future golden age when there will be a paradise of beauty for all who are alive; and two other visions of the golden age involving figures well known to Hindus, namely Narayan and Lakshmi, and **Krishna** and Radha. The paintings also include a vision of the subtle region beyond the material world and of the soul-world beyond that; a vision of Lekhraj himself as the Father of humanity; and the last painting depicts a more sombre vision of mass destruction involving explosions and the crumbling of buildings.

These visions are explained before I am led into a gigantic auditorium that can hold 3,000 people and is one of the largest in Asia in the late 1980s. It is called Om Shanti Bhavan. There are numerous illustrations at the front, including one of Dada Lekhraj meditating in lotus position with God above him, in the form of a spark of light radiating light from within himself. Another of Dada Lekhraj with Mama, Om Radhe, the first administrative head of the Brahma Kumaris. Yet another is of a host of leading figures of the great religious traditions of the world, and finally another depicts heaven on earth as it will be in the golden age. In the great hall there are earphones and translation facilities from Hindi into French, English, German, Kannada, Portuguese, Tamil and Telugu. There are also seven televisions, a number of well-equipped audio-visual rooms, and urns of flowers all around. This is where the 6am meditation sessions and other large gatherings take place.

If I am under the impression that Madhuban is just a huge auditorium with large sets of attached living quarters, I am soon disabused of that perception. Madhuban comprises more than forty departments, serviced by some 200 people who look after the needs of Madhuban and its many visitors. There is a tailoring department, where all the clothes of the community are made; kitchens, which are able to feed up to 3,000 people at a time; an electrical department; an oil- and soap-making department; storerooms for rice, wheat, vegetables and spices; a milk and yoghurt room; and a chapati-making department. There is also a general store; three large dining halls; a pot-cleaning area; a printing and copying office; a welding shed; a carpentry department; a dispensary; a fruit department; meditation and meeting halls; a post office; and a cash-dispensing centre.

At 4.15pm it is time for tea, and at 5.00pm there is a class teaching the main tenets of the Brahma Kumaris and their principles. Dinner at 7.30pm is followed, at 8.30pm, by another class on what is happening to Brahma Kumaris around the world. At 10pm it is time for bed, prior to being woken at 3.45am. At 4am many will gather in the great auditorium to meditate silently. After a short rest, there will be further meditation (as in Edinburgh) from 6am to 7.30am in the great auditorium, and the message for the day, known as the murli, will be read. After breakfast at 8am the main work period for the community commences, followed by another class from 10.30am to 12.30pm.

Life at Madhuban sounds hectic, and in a sense it certainly is. Yet there is a sense of happiness and peace pervading the purposeful activity. Busy it may be, frenetic it is not. But what about my efforts to understand them?

* * * *

Although I have read a good deal of the literature by the Brahma Kumaris or about them, the personal experiences distilled in these vignettes have been essential to my 'getting inside' what it means to be a Brahma Kumari. An American Indian proverb suggests that to understand others fully it is necessary to walk a couple of miles in their moccasins. I trust that the four vignettes in this introduction have whetted the appetites of readers to 'pass over' into understanding the world-view of the Brahma Kumaris — critically yet empathetically.

1

Dada Lekhraj and the Sindi background of the Brahma Kumaris

A Snapshot of Dada Lekhraj

The history of the Brahma Kumaris begins with the Indian gentleman featured on the large photograph in the Edinburgh centre and on the large paintings in the Mount Abu building. His original name was Lekhraj Khubchand but he was affectionately known as Dada Lekhraj. The basic details of his early life can be quickly summarised. His home was in Hyderabad in the region of Sind in north-west India, where he was a self-made businessman first in wheat and then in the diamond trade. Born in 1876, much of his life followed a reasonably predictable, prosperous and pious course. His father was a teacher, and although his own formal education was not strong he read and wrote fluently in Sindi and Hindi, his English was good, and he was self-taught in literature and art. His diamond business prospered to the extent that he became a millionaire (see illus. 1.1). His reputation for piety also grew, and by 1936 he was a well-respected lay Hindu, with advice from spiritual preceptors, with a penchant for charitable activities, a propensity for going on pilgrimages, and a facility in sacred texts such as the Hindu ***Bhagavad Gītā*** and the Sikh ***Guru Granth Sahib***. He enjoyed entertaining ***sadhus*** and other kinds of **gurus** and holy men, and he took pleasure in the social activities appropriate to his status as a senior diamond merchant. On the face of it his life had been successful and relatively uneventful.

When Dada Lekhraj was nearing sixty years old his wife proposed that they should both enter the third (and less active) stage of life and begin to disengage from householder and business activities. His response was that he was ready to retire — but not yet. He suggested that, first, he should continue working for two to four years, and hopefully double his fortune, which then could be dispensed to the poor and used for other good works;

1.1: Dada Lekhraj, formerly a diamond merchant, in the 1930s.

after that he would retire. This plan was to be overtaken when Dada Lekhraj began to have visions. And as a result of these he was transported into a completely new lifestyle, which was to last until his death in 1969 at the age of ninety-three. Incidentally, it is highly unusual for religious leaders to emerge unheralded in their ageing years. The charisma and promise of great figures such as the Buddha, Jesus and Muhammad all flared in their youth or early middle age.

From the Brahma Kumari viewpoint the early life of their founder, although of some interest, was relatively unimportant. The key events of his life happened in and after 1936, when Dada Lekhraj passed into a new stage of existence and the world was also deemed to move into a new state. The Brahma Kumaris believed in the importance of the new age that was developing, not the old one that was passing away. This is understandable. After all, if Dada Lekhraj had had no visions, and if his life had continued its previous course, few people would remember him now except for his family and friends.

And yet Dada Lekhraj's early background in Sind is important when attempting to understand him and the movement that came into being as a result of his experience. It is therefore crucial to see him within the context of his Sindi roots. For around sixty years he had been formed by Sindi society, culture and religion, although he broke away from some of those roots in a spectacular way. Moreover the Sindi Hindu tradition in which he had been brought up was deeply affected from 1947 to 1951 by the tragic events accompanying the independence and partition of India. Many of the Sindi Hindus became displaced persons in the new nation of India, while Sind was transformed into a predominantly Muslim state within the new nation of Pakistan. Fortunately, this dispersion worked to the advantage of the Brahma Kumaris in 1950, when they moved from Pakistan to Mount Abu in India, because they came into contact with various groups of Sindis scattered around India. This opened a window of opportunity for the expansion of the movement, and from India it would expand into the wider world.

A Brief History of Sind

Geographically, Sind is a separate area in north-west India bounded by mountains to the north-west, the great Thar desert to the east, the Rann of Kutch to the south and the Arabian Sea to the south-west. The original inhabitants of Sind, from *c.*2500–1700 BCE, appear to have been the people of the Indus Valley civilisation, the ruins of which were discovered in 1922 and included figurines of goddesses, and a prototype seal of the later Hindu deity **Shiva**. It is intriguing that the importance of the female element in religion, and the notion of Shiva as the supreme transcendent soul, are also fundamental elements in Brahma Kumari thinking today.

There is some evidence that the Indus Valley civilisation was over-run by the Aryans *c.*1500 BCE. They built up the earliest form of what is now called the Hindu tradition and began to set down in writing their sacred texts known collectively as the **Veda.** In Sind what was later called the Sindi Hindu tradition had begun. A series of other invasions included that by Darius of Persia (522–486 BCE), and subsequent ones by Parthians, Scythians and Kushans. These, and the rise of the Buddhist and Jain traditions in the sixth century BCE, had little long-term effect. The invasion that had more lasting consequences was by the Muslims in 711 CE. The region was then nominally ruled by Muslims until 1843, when the British took over Sind. However, in 1857 even nominal Muslim rule collapsed throughout India when the Muslim association with the first War of Indian Independence (otherwise known as the Indian Mutiny) resulted in virtually the whole of India coming under British rule.

Thus Dada Lekhraj, although a Hindu by background, lived his early life in a region that was predominantly Muslim. By the time that he was twenty-five, in 1901, the Sind census showed that there were 2,446,459 Muslims and 751,252 Hindus in Sind. Ten years later, in 1911, the Hyderabad census recorded 781,219 Muslims and 245,941 Hindus in Hyderabad.

Fortunately, Dada Lekhraj and other Hindus were able to flourish reasonably well under the hegemony of the British, and the British made Dada Lekhraj's own city of Hyderabad the capital of Sind. How then did he flourish, and how did he fall out of favour with his own community?

Sind Culture

Even before the end of Muslim power in India, Hindus had grown in stature. In Sind, for example, a Hindu class of government servants named **Amils** had filled government jobs, had engaged in professional services and had become proficient in trade.

Dada Lekhraj was born into a branch of the Kripalani family, one of the four well-known Hindu families in Sind — the surnames of other three being Mahtani, Mirchandani and Vaswani. His full name was Lekhraj Khubchand Kripalani. He went into trade, and the new circumstances in Sind favoured the success of his business. He became part of a wider 'Sind Worki' merchant community centred on Hyderabad, which included craft skills involving *lungis*, calico, silk and gold and silver thread, inlaid gold- and silverware, lacquer and pottery.

For people with entrepreneurial vision the British Empire opened up vast opportunities, and the businesses of fellow merchants such as Mr Pohumal and Mr Vasiamal were able to flourish as far away as Egypt and the Straits Settlements. Dada Lekhraj established houses, shops and offices in Kolkata and Mumbai as well as Hyderabad, and he eventually became a millionaire.

Although Sind was his base, he was able to wander in imagination beyond India into the wider world. His success was built on a technical skill with diamonds; it was also helped by his natural charm and skill with people. Later on, his business acumen and easy social abilities were to stand Dada Lekhraj in good stead after he experienced his important spiritual call.

Social Life in Sind

As well as the geographical and cultural background of Sind, its social background was also important in influencing the early life of Dada Lekhraj. The two main elements in Sindi Hindu society that were of relevance to his life were the caste system and the position of women. Although he and the early Brahma Kumaris were to complain about the deleterious effects of the caste system and about the lowly position of women, ironically Sind was better off in these two respects than many other parts of India. This brings to mind Cobban's famous theory of revolution — that revolution happens when things are getting better, not when they are at their worst (Cobban, 1968). The Brahma Kumari 'revolution' occurred when the Sind situation was improving.

Dada Lekhraj's main local milieu was the Bhaibund community, which was part of a wider Lohana 'trading caste' in Sind. The **Lohanas** who formed the mass of the population were an all-absorbing caste which gave shelter to various elements of population from the adjoining province. The customs of marrying inside (endogamy) or outside (exogamy) the local community, clan or tribe were less rigid in Sind compared with most of Hindu India, and social relations were marked by a degree of freedom. For example, it appears that Dada Lekhraj was able to mix relatively freely with people who were of a higher caste and social status, and he had good relations with some of the rajahs and maharajahs of various Indian native states, including the kings of Nepal and Valaipur. One of Lekhraj's daughters-in-law, B. K. Brijindra, states:

> The maharajahs, the wealthy clients, and the business leaders with whom he was in contact used to visit Dada as his guests, and their arrival coincided with the time Dada had to do his *puja* (worship), but Dada would not postpone or cut short these religious activities. Moreover he would not compromise his living style (Chander, 1983b, p. 29).

His VIP guests were unaccustomed to such simplicity and absence of hedonism in their dining habits, and they used to joke that 'Dada's parties are certainly without flair'. This anecdote also points to Dada Lekhraj's religious piety.

What then of the place of women in Sindi Hindu society at the beginning of the twentieth century? An analysis of their status is necessary in order to understand the promotion of women into the top leadership posts within the Brahma Kumaris.

In two respects Hindu women in Sind held a reasonable position compared with their sex elsewhere in India. Because they were surrounded by Muslims, the various Hindu castes lived fairly inter-dependent lives and had a reasonable sense of social cohesion from which women benefited. They gained, too, from the Sindi notion of the importance of virgin girls within society. A local saying was that a virgin, known often as a ***devi*** (goddess), was equal to a hundred **Brahmins**. Her chastity could be seen in terms of sacred energy and special power. Thus before marriage a Sindi Hindu woman had a reasonable sense of freedom and status, and this was enhanced by the fact that there were more males than females within the Lohana community. At the 1931 census, for example, there were 246,243 Lohana males and 213,115 females. Women therefore had a scarcity value.

These advantages were tempered by three traditions that some deemed to be disadvantages for women. First, the Sindi Hindu community remained a patriarchal society. Each Hindu family, which was usually a joint family, lived under the authority of the man of the family. All the individuals in the family were managed by him. He was their spokesman and representative in community and other matters. He was the person who organised the financial affairs and religious ceremonies of the family. It was he who was responsible for household discipline and educational matters. When the father of the house died responsibility passed on to the eldest son, who lit his father's funeral pyre and took over management of the household.

Secondly, on marriage, a Sindi Hindu girl entered the household of her husband and came under the general aegis of her father-in-law. She became the helpmate of her husband and, in the first instance, became of service to him. Once she bore children her status was enhanced and she became ***shakti*** (power personified). She gained greater status in internal family matters and sometimes in practical religious matters. Popular Hinduism owes much to the role of women in its practical outworkings. However a woman was ancillary to her husband, and if she became a widow her status declined. She had no independent existence in her own right. She was valued, or otherwise, as a married member of a wider family.

Thirdly, religious celibacy was not a real possibility for women, and it was a prerogative almost wholly confined to men. In some religious groups among the Hindus, and with the **Udasis** among the Sikhs, men could bypass the 'duty' of marriage and become lifelong celibates (***sannyasis***). Furthermore, men who had fulfilled the sacrament of marriage were more able in later life to retreat from the world with honour and acclaim. The third stage of life, proposed by his wife Jashoda to Dada Lekhraj, which involved their semi-retirement from the affairs of the world, could be a joint venture. However the final stage of life, involving more complete retirement, was in practice largely restricted to men. To all intents and purposes women were therefore excluded from religious celibacy, and this was a serious matter for the Brahma Kumaris.

This general subservience of women to men was heightened by another factor especially present in the Sindi experience. The greater freedom opened up by the trading success of Sindi Hindu men, which took them around India and into farther parts of the world, was good for women in that it brought them the fruits of growing wealth and status. However it also underlined their own subordinate position and their confinement to their own community. In practice, many Sindi women spent most of their time in the house, while visits outside the home were often limited to religious gatherings and to family ceremonials of one sort or another. Moreover their educational opportunities were minimal, and there was therefore little solace in that direction. Also, their husbands were away on businesses for months or even longer: Dada Lekhraj, for example, had businesses in Kolkata and Mumbai that necessitated periodic visits there. Women therefore felt they had married absentee husbands. This factor was exacerbated by a third factor that is often commented on in Brahma Kumari literature: while the Sindi husbands were away for extended periods of time, they were suspected of having extra-marital affairs in the places where they visited.

In so far as some Sindi women harboured suspicions about their husbands' sexual extra-marital relationships, the insensitivity of some husbands when they returned from their journeys increased the tension. Their wives, deprived of sex through the absence of their husbands, found that they were perceived to be the sexual 'property' of their returned 'masters' and 'deities'. Many Hindu women accepted this overall scenario as the way things were. However a significant minority felt restlessness and their morale was low because of the combination of the contradictions mentioned above, and so these Hindu wives were to be particularly receptive to the message of the Brahma Kumaris.

Why did Dada Lekhraj feel so strongly about the situation of women in Sind? After all, he was a benign and caring yet sometimes absentee Sindi husband, and was no doubt aware of the factors outlined above and sensed the unfairness. Two or three incidents from his earlier life show that he was unhappy about the position of women in Sindi society long before he had his visions.

When the time came for one of his daughters — affectionately known as Puttu — to be married, he helped her to choose as a husband a relatively lowly man called Bodhraj, who was the young headmaster of a local school, instead of a more rich and accomplished person. His decision triggered debate and wonderment in local circles, but his concern was for his daughter as a person. A second unusual incident sheds further light on Dada Lekhraj's feelings about the position of women. He was devoted to the Hindu deity Vishnu in the form of Narayan, and in the bazaars of India then, as now, coloured pictures of the gods were a common sight. One such picture portrayed Narayan as a majestic Hindu deity being served in a condescending way by his female consort Lakshmi, who was massaging his legs. This did not seem right to Dada Lekhraj and so he commissioned a revised picture in which Narayan and Lakshmi are portrayed as equals. Thirdly, Dada Lekhraj's business was in diamonds and jewellery, and this brought him into relatively intimate contact with a number of women who were the recipients of his creations. A typical contact with a princely home was described by B. K. Brijindra, his daughter-in-law: 'When Dada came, the Rajmata — the Queen Mother — herself would call him in to show the diamonds to her daughters and daughters-in-law' (Chander, 1983b, pp. 26–7). His general character and sensitivity seem to have given Dada Lekhraj an intuitive concern for the needs of women; this not only helped his business dealings but also gave premonitions of his seemingly surprising decision later in life to give women the leading role in the movement he founded.

Dada Lekhraj's Early Religious Life

Dada Lekhraj's religion was part of his life. Indeed it is remarkable how his religion and his life formed a whole when he was a rich merchant, and this combination worked equally well when he moved on to a life of spiritual simplicity. Up to the age of around sixty, he was seemingly a devoted practising Sindi Hindu who was well-to-do, devout and also a respected merchant. It is hard to find obvious indicators of his later fame and notoriety from this earlier life. Indeed those who knew him in his younger days remark both on his character and piety — and on his ordinariness.

From his father Dada Lekhraj inherited the Vallabhachari religious tradition, which was based on the work of Vallabha (1479–1531) and focused on the Hindu deity Krishna. In some ways Dada Lekhraj's position was to be similar to Vallabha's. According to Vallabhachari tradition, Vallabha was sitting one night by the river Jumna worrying about the state of the world in the final and most desperate age of the earth (***kali yuga***) when he received a vision of Krishna and heard Krishna speaking to him. In response, Vallabha said that for thousands of years he had been separated from his beloved Lord Krishna and that this had robbed him not only of the pangs of separation which a healthy soul, as a rule, ought to feel but also of the infinite joy he had had in his company. Thus Vallabha laid down at Krishna's lotus-feet his body, sense organs, vital breath and mind, together with their various functions. He also promised his own self as well as his beloved, his house, his progeny, his relations and his wealth, together with his worldly as well as other-worldly belongings. Henceforth Vallabha would be the humble servant of Krishna. His life would be devoted to him for ever.

It is not difficult to see similarities between this vision of Vallabha and those Dada Lekhraj was soon to have. There is the same concern for the desperate state of the world, the need for the soul to renew deep contact with God after years of separation, the absolute surrender to God and the sense of living for God in the world.

Although happy and successful, Dada Lekhraj was not static in his thoughts or aspirations. His life was in process; he was on a journey. He was inquisitive and always ready to ask questions as he was not content with blind dogma. Thus when at the pilgrimage place of Amarnath he saw an image of the Lord Shiva formed out of ice he asked the presiding priest (***pujari***) whether the Shiva image had been a natural shape or one made by human hands.

Dada Lekhraj had a succession of twelve spiritual preceptors, and he gave each guru his undivided attention. When he felt that there was no more to be learnt he passed on to another guru — until at last he realised that he must go beyond gurus altogether.

His religious practice took a number of other forms. He was fond of pilgrimages, and while a travelling merchant he visited various holy sites — Hardwar, Amarnath and Banaras (Varanasi). He also knew Allahabad and Vrindaban. When on these pilgrimages, and at other times, he took his favourite text, the *Bhagavad Gītā* — it was his guide to life. Like his contemporary Mahatma Gandhi, Dada Lekhraj pondered long and hard on this sacred work. It helped to reveal the road to his spiritual experiences, and when these experiences came he saw the *Bhagavad Gītā* as still being important but in a different way.

In his family life Dada Lekhraj practised his religion in the time-honoured way: he married, became a householder and with his wife Jashoda had six children (four girls and two boys). He was affectionate towards Jashoda, and kind and concerned in the general welfare of his family. In his children he instilled ethical principles through reason and persuasion.

In his business life Dada Lekhraj was a good Hindu in two ways. He practised ***artha*** (making a living) — the second life-aim for Hindus — as well as ***dharma*** (the moral, humane and religious side of life), the third life-aim. His *artha*, as a diamond merchant, came from his considerable technical expertise in valuing and knowing diamonds. However he had, if anything, a deeper regard for *dharma*. His own lifestyle was not ostentatious. He was a vegetarian. He avoided alcohol and smoking. His clothes, although neat, were not lavish. His success in business however did not mould his lifestyle; instead, his *dharma* pervaded his business. His hospitality was warm to visitors, whether rajahs or visiting holy men, whom he would entertain and engage in discussion. Inside and outside the family Dada Lekhraj strove to be charitable.

A Transformation

This exemplary, upright Hindu first had visions around the sixtieth year of his life. Even before this there is evidence that Dada Lekhraj was already becoming more introspective. His wife Jashoda's suggestion that he and she together should go into meditative retirement may well have been a sensitive prod for him to follow a path he had already begun to tread. At a time when Dada Lekhraj was thinking of and planning retirement, a flood of ecstatic experiences came on him. In place of retirement there was increased activity. But it was to be activity of a different kind as the force and traumatic effect of his new spiritual experiences transformed Dada Lekhraj's life. He was to enter a kind of traumatic yet golden spiritual wilderness or, as he was to call it, undergo a period of intense preparation for the future. He was to be led along a path, the ways and ends of which were not immediately clear, but they resulted in the rise of a new religious movement — the Brahma Kumaris.

2

Dada Lekhraj's Visions and the beginning of the Brahma Kumaris

The striking thing about Dada Lekhraj's visions is that they were new, they were original and they could not have been anticipated. When they began in 1936 his notion of working on after the age of sixty to increase his vast fortune evaporated. His amazing experiences were not only of deep spiritual importance but also frightening. He described wires of light shooting into him from a point that spoke, and a powerful fire burning in his bones. Thereafter, Dada Lekhraj lost interest in diamonds, business and money as he realised that he no longer had control over his own life. He seemed to need only the grace and silence of the figure of Narayan, and meditation in the early mornings.

As the visions came to someone who was not adept in dreams, visions or spiritual experiences, they were traumatic and psychologically shattering. Dada Lekhraj found it hard to put into words the deepest and most startling things that were happening to him: that God Himself was telling him to create a new world — that he was to be God's tool — that he, though not God, was God's chosen. What was happening to his life? How could he understand it? What were the consequences for himself, his family and for others? Being a sensible man, and knowledgeable about the world, Dada Lekhraj knew that even if he could not interpret what it all meant there would be a price to pay as well as a reward to be gained.

The Brahma Kumaris, and to some extend Dada Lekhraj himself, were later to present these vivid experiences in a more natural and positive light — and this is understandable. A tradition needed to be established in straightforward and clear terms. There would then come into play what Max Weber (1964) used to call the 'routinisation of charisma': in this process, charismatic experiences are put into a framework of understanding, and an organisation is built on the basis of them.

Specific Visions

Six specific experiences stand out in a series of inner events. The first happened one day when Dada Lekhraj was meeting some fellow disciples of his spiritual counsellor. They were in his bungalow and he felt an unusual sensation coming over him so that he had to leave the room. While resting alone he had a sense of being overcome by bliss, and of going beyond the consciousness of his body. He felt himself to be a pure soul floating, as it were, on an ocean of bliss, and he also had a vision of Vishnu.

Not long afterwards Dada Lekhraj was staying in Banaras on business. When meditating in the summerhouse of a friend he again had a deep inner experience. He had the same sense as in the previous vision of leaving the body, of remembering God and of becoming light. He wrote five letters home and his daughter-in-law Brijindra describes how, when the letters arrived, they seemed to vibrate in her hand in accordance with the sensations they were attempting to communicate.

Later on, during the same Banaras visit, Dada Lekhraj had a compelling twofold vision. One part of it was benign, the other awful. Alongside an abundance of wealth there was excessive suffering including some cataclysmic destructions. Dada Lekhraj looked at such real horror, pain, misery, blood and fire that he could hardly bear it. He felt that he could see the big cities of Europe and America with their gleaming towering buildings toppling, with great holes gaping in their walls, with the sky black, with the ground a brilliant acid orange, and with streets and towns on fire. These included his own streets and cities — in Kolkata, Delhi and Mumbai, as well as Hyderabad, Madras, Banaras and Lucknow — all over his beloved India. He fell into a cold sweat, tears seared his cheeks, and his hands almost tore hair from his head. He was found by his friend, who had been woken by Dada Lekhraj's screams coming from the little summerhouse on that hot Banaras night.

What then was the benign counterpart to this apocalyptic vision? What were the glorious elements in the experience? Dada Lekhraj recollected tiny stars floating in a beautiful light, shining not like stars in the sky but like ones in our hearts and eyes. They moved down slowly and floated above his head. They appeared to be living 'sparks' that turned, as they came close to earth, into living beings — beings of a beauty, divinity and grace that took his breath away. They smiled and moved in a courtly dance before him. They beckoned to him, and were dressed in rich gossamer clothes, diamonds and jewels of rosy light. Dada Lekhraj felt that whatever and wherever this place was he would like to go and stay there.

Beneath the ecstasy and the turmoil of these visions Dada Lekhraj's perturbation was real. What did these visions mean? How could they be interpreted? Where were they taking him? He travelled to Kolkata and looked at the trappings of his great shop in the light of his new experiences. His diamond business was now meaningless so he approached his partner who agreed to buy him out. He then wired his family to tell them what had happened. We can imagine their confusion. Had he really got rid of his great business in the twinkling of an eye? What was going on? Dada Lekhraj arrived back in Sind a changed person.

Three more explicit visions were still to befall him. Alone in his office he heard that his uncle had died, and he had a vision of what had happened at the death of his uncle. He saw his uncle's life energies moving up his body and being centred in his head. Suddenly he saw his uncle's soul leaving his body, exiting by way of his forehead. He knew that it was only his uncle's body that had died. His soul was still alive.

Shortly afterwards, Dada Lekhraj had a vision of the four-armed Hindu deity Vishnu who seemed to come through an opening in the darkness glowing delicate and bright, looking gentle yet almost blinding. His four arms seemed totally natural and his dark eyes very deep. He seemed to be just standing there with light around him, showing himself, and making Lekhraj know who he was. In his perplexity Dada Lekhraj went to his spiritual guide — his guru — to gain enlightenment concerning the meaning of his experience. Indeed he was hoping to understand the gamut of experiences he was undergoing. He was in an existentially exalted yet vulnerable situation. He greeted his preceptor in the time-honoured manner, and described his wonderful experience of Vishnu in the supposition that his guru might somehow have been involved in communicating it to him. It quickly became clear that his preceptor had no notion of what he was talking about — indeed the guru was perplexed. Far from giving advice his reactions suggested that he himself had questions about the experience, that he was fearful concerning it, that he was limited in his imagination about it and that he was stereotyped in his response. More in sorrow than in anger Dada Lekhraj realised that he must let his spiritual preceptor go. He could be of little help. Only God could be of help now.

Dada Lekhraj's final and most climactic vision occurred one evening at his home. It was even deeper than the others. He felt that God was speaking directly in and through him. It was witnessed by his wife and daughter-in-law, whereas the other visions had been experienced alone. Words played an important part on this occasion, while previously the visions had been mainly pictorial. As far as Dada Lekhraj was concerned it confirmed his new calling. It was, in effect, the launch pad for the Brahma Kumari tradition.

There is a slight discrepancy between his own account of the circumstances of this vision, and that given by his daughter-in-law Brijindra. She related how Dada Lekhraj was at a congregational meeting addressed by his guru, but suddenly left — a matter of disrespect in the Indian context. His wife Jashoda and Brijindra followed Dada Lekhraj, as something was clearly happening to him. Dada Lekhraj's own account made no mention of walking out of the meeting, and his reflection simply stated that it was in an evening after the visitors had left the house. He concentrated on the vision itself. He may therefore have left the meeting as stated in Brijindra's account and neglected to mention it in his own version because it no longer seemed important as he had already come to the conclusion that his guru was of limited worth. The vividness of his experience, corroborated by Brijindra's version, is brought out in his own reminiscence. Unfortunately, it is not dated so we do not know how long after the event it was written. We are not aware therefore whether later thoughts and experiences have been interpreted back into it. Nevertheless, its immediacy speaks for itself.

While upstairs in his room, Dada Lekhraj described how a deep peace settled on him, and on the whole house. It was a powerful and hushed presence, a vibration that spoke in the silence and seemed to bring awe and wonder, a presence that was not human. He related how his wife and daughter seemed to have felt it too. However he ceased to be aware of them or of anything except the long lines of light shooting into him, like white hot wires, from a totally concentrated point of focus. He felt transfixed by their current, which seemed to run right through him and glow almost unbearably hot. Dada Lekhraj went on to describe that the form, burning brightly and powerfully, also had a soft and delicate centre, like a father or mother or child. That form moved down on him, and in on him. Although staring at the people in the room, his eyes could see nothing except this deep glow, a pervading rod of light, a subtle energy of life itself, a living being entering his heart and soul. His mind wanted to cry out aloud but at the same time he was dragged gently into a depthless ocean of totally cooling peace. Dada Lekhraj mentioned how a light seemed to come from his face and eyes, head, and nose and ears, and when he opened his mouth to speak it was as if he spoke with words carved out of red gold light. He had a sense that the Hindu deity Shiva was there showing himself, and promising that he would reveal more. He felt as if he had been bathed like a newborn child in the depths of a baptism of water and fire, of knowledge and light. He had, so to speak, been cradled in bliss.

In her account Brijindra confirmed that Dada Lekhraj's eyes and face became red and how she herself felt bodiless and light while looking at him. She heard sounds and words coming from his mouth but it was as though someone else was speaking through him. She commented that she could not forget that voice nor that scene. The atmosphere was electric, more than real, and her condition of feeling without a body had remained alive in her memory.

It is of course impossible to reconstruct visions, so they have to be put into words by the recipient and by people observing the recipient. The very fact of describing visions however distorts them to some extent. This would be true even if the account was written immediately. In practice, most visions including Dada Lekhraj's are described later, and they are unwittingly or otherwise put into a framework of interpretation. Paradoxically, any difference in detail between separate accounts adds to the authenticity. If a completely watertight and packaged account had been intended, differences of detail could have been eradicated.

After his final vision, Dada Lekhraj knew that he was not mad, and that an important revelation and task had been given to him. But he still had to work out in detail what it was. He needed to find a meaning for the varied content of his different visions: of Vishnu; the destruction of the world; the sparks descending as living deities; the sense of being bodiless and light; the vision of Vishnu as a spark of incandescent light; and that of Shiva. How did they fit together?

To add to the sense of all-impending change, without him necessarily welcoming it, people had begun to gather in Dada Lekhraj's presence, fascinated by the vibrations that were emanating from him. There was a combination of semi-chaos and expectancy that heralded the dawn of a new movement.

The Rise of a Community

Dada Lekhraj set up a series of regular meetings (***satsangs***) in his home to discuss and seek truth. These began as a family *satsang*, which friends and neighbours could attend. More distant relatives heard about it and came as well. Dada Lekhraj led these meetings until his visit to Kashmir in July 1936, and he did so again when he got back. Finally, stories about his visions and teaching spread more extensively, and sundry people were attracted out of curiosity. By that time Dada Lekhraj had virtually stopped leaving his home, which was later called Om Niwas and had become the meeting place for a floating congregation.

Initially, Dada Lekhraj himself was the attraction at the meetings. He had given up his business suddenly and without warning, and this had been unusual. However there was also a change in him inwardly. When people went near him they often claimed to be able to feel vibrations of love and power and warmth. Moreover Dada Lekhraj had begun to teach.

The attention was both welcome and unwelcome to Dada Lekhraj. It was clear to him and others that he was a focal point for the new work, yet he felt that he was a vehicle for God and that the point lay in God. He was not a human guru attracting followers. He was a means whereby people could find God and themselves. At the same time, Dada Lekhraj felt that he had a special role as a human being, but not as a divine figure.

It is not unknown in India even now for men to give up their jobs and go away to spend time in study or meditation, and eventually to teach. With Dada Lekhraj the whole process was telescoped. It began almost immediately after his visions, without a long period of study and reflection, and he taught from his own home in the midst of his own family.

Dada Lekhraj hit on the classical teaching method of starting with the familiar in order to go beyond it to something that was in some respects startlingly new. He took as his basis the *Bhagavad Gītā*, his favourite Hindu text. He felt that he was being given ***Gītā Gyān***, fundamental knowledge about the *Bhagavad Gītā*. He also perceived that there were some similarities between his own visions of the coming of a new world and the destruction of the old world, and the vision of Krishna to Arjuna in the *Bhagavad Gītā* in his benign and awful forms. Therefore Dada Lekhraj held to the teachings of the *Gītā* in so far as they accorded with what he had been vouchsafed, and he adapted them in new directions when they departed from what he felt had been revealed to him. In this way he was able to teach regularly, to build up a pattern of thought, and to integrate the new insights he was continually receiving from God.

Probably more important initially than his teachings and the worldview he was starting to formulate was the spiritual experience that seemed to affect those who attended the *satsang*. There was a sense of vibratory power when its members recited together the sacred phrase 'Om'. (Om is a very ancient holy syllable and a powerful Hindu word.) Indeed at an early phase in the life of the *satsang* Dada Lekhraj became known as Om Baba. In response to his presence and his teachings people began to have visions along the same lines as his own: of Krishna, of the golden age to come, and so on. There seem to have been a considerable number of visions in those early days, and the *satsang* became known as the place where you were likely to have such experiences. This sense of aesthetic and charismatic spirituality was important. It was immediate. The significance and worldview were developing, and the outlines of a body of knowledge were also emerging. These were based on the central features of the visions and were refined and expanded later.

Some of the Early Followers

Many of the people who began to attend the *satsang* were women, and a number of them became leading figures in the new movement. Three in particular possessed abilities that were to be of considerable use in the future directions of the *satsang*. Their names were Brijindra (Dada Lekhraj's daughter-in-law), Radha (who became the first administrative leader of the new movement) and Nirmal Shanta (Dada Lekhraj's eldest daughter).

Brijindra

Born into a wealthy Indian family living in Hyderabad, in early adolescence Brijindra married one of Dada Lekhraj's sons and moved over to live with the Lekhraj family. This involved a slight change in lifestyle because her father's home had been more westernised than that of her father-in-law, Dada Lekhraj.

Brijindra was present during Dada Lekhraj's climactic vision. Strangely enough, although visions abounded among some of the early followers, she was not vouchsafed one. She was aware from his demeanour and teachings that her father-in-law now viewed each person as a soul rather than as a mere body, but did not realise the full significance of this until one day she met him on a staircase. As they passed each other, and their gazes met, his ***drishti*** (gaze) penetrated Brijindra's soul and she realised that her father-in-law had a new persona. She had a sense of awakening to the reality of her own being as a soul.

She played an important part in the early days of the Brahma Kumaris, and when the movement transferred to Karachi she lived in the same bungalow as its key figure — her father-in-law. She was responsible for recording some of the messages that came to him in the form of murlis, and for passing them on to others in chronicled accounts. Later on, after the move to Mount Abu, Brijindra spearheaded the work of the Brahma Kumaris in Mumbai and the rest of Maharashtra state, and took other leadership responsibilities before and after the death of Dada Lekhraj.

Radha

The jewel in the crown among the early visitors to the *satsang* was a young woman called Radha Pokardas Vaswani. She had a beautiful singing voice, black hair and dancing eyes, a powerful yet compassionate personality and a first-class brain. She seemed to understand immediately the importance of the teachings that were being offered at Om Niwas. Remaining celibate and taking up raja-yoga meditation came easily to her. During her early visits to the *satsang* she wrote a song:

> O friends what shall I show you?
> And how can I show you what I saw,
> What I saw in Om Mandli?
> O friends, how can I describe such joy?
> The voice of Om.
>
> Like an arrow pierced my mind,
> And calm and quiet I became,
> And all my troubles, all my stories,
> All my sorrows died away.
> (Chander, 1983b, p. 60)

Before Radha even came to a *satsang* Dada Lekhraj's wife had sensed in a vision that Radha would have a prime leadership position in the new movement. She had quickly shown gifts of teaching and administration. Before long they would be more deeply used. Radha's qualities of personality and leadership were such that even her own mother referred to her as 'Mama', meaning mother.

Radha became captivated by the resonance of the Om syllable, so she was designated 'Om Radhe'. Later she was given another new name — Jagadamba Saraswati. Although this was a name for the Hindu goddess of knowledge, in the case of Radha it referred, in theory and in practice, to her mastery of the knowledge that was being given at the *satsang*. Alongside the male founder of the *satsang*, a complementary female leader seemed naturally to be emerging.

Nirmal Shanta

The story of Dada Lekhraj's eldest daughter was more poignant. Her story spills over into some of the reasons for the opposition to the rise of the Brahma Kumaris. Her father had married her into a wealthy Sindi family, and in 1936 she was living in the house of her in-laws in the midst of great wealth and luxury. Her father-in-law was a ***mukhi***, a politically important person in the city of Hyderabad.

She inevitably heard about the rise of the *satsang* at her father's home. When she went over there she could see that something had happened to her father and mother, who viewed everyone as souls. They had accumulated what amounted to a new 'family' through the medium of the *satsang*, and they encouraged Nirmal Shanta (as she became known) to go along the new path they had begun to tread.

Then, back at home, one night she woke up three times. On each occasion she had a vision of her father as Om Baba and on the third occasion Krishna was with him. Her father said to her: 'Daughter wake up, you have to do the work of world upliftment' (Chander, 1983b, p. 65). At sunset her father came to her in person and she told him what had happened. She knew that the whole episode signalled for her a new kind of life.

This indeed turned out to be the case. Nirmal Shanta eventually led the Brahma Kumari work in Kolkata and in the Eastern zone around that city. However there were other consequences too. The new name she had adopted — Nirmal — meant 'purity'. However her alignment to a movement that stressed purity and celibacy was not acceptable to her husband and father-in-law, and opposition in particular by her father-in-law, an influential man, to the Brahma Kumaris was to have practical as well as emotional consequences.

3

Growth of the Brahma Kumaris and opposition to them

The Retreat to Kashmir

At times of crisis and decision-making many great religious leaders have felt the need to seek seclusion. Examples come to mind of Jesus in the wilderness, Muhammad in the caves outside Mecca, Saint Paul after the vision on the road to Damascus and the Buddha after the flight from his palace. However Dada Lekhraj — or Om Baba as he was coming to be known — did not go into solitary isolation. He took his family with him. In July 1936 they travelled from Hyderabad to Kashmir, and in their absence the *satsang* was left to look after itself. Although not fully spelled out in Brahma Kumari literature, the reasons for the retreat to Kashmir appear to be for physical, spiritual and mental renewal.

Om Baba needed to reflect on his remaining life's work. He wanted time to shepherd his physical energies in isolation, away from the increasingly urgent attentions of the members of the *satsang*. Both for his own sake and that of the wider movement, he also wished to deepen his spiritual energies. These included spiritual experiences such as dreams and visions as well as doing more meditation using raja yoga. Furthermore, Om Baba needed to think more about the vision of destruction — what was it? Was it a parable about purifying the soul, was it a premonition of the Second World War that was looming, or was it a prophesy of a nuclear holocaust? Equally, the central insight into the distinction between body-consciousness and soul-consciousness could be interpreted differently. In practice, celibacy loomed large in the analysis of this distinction, and yet the inter-connection still needed to be worked out. The whole pattern of knowledge that underpinned the experience of the *satsang* was still to be cast into its final form.

The retreat to Kashmir also provided an opportunity for Om Baba's physical family to review their own situation. The opposition by Nirmal Shanta's father-in-law had revealed latent tensions within the family since Om Baba's traumatic experiences. If families were not able to understand the motivation and impetus behind the *satsang*, were members of the *satsang* to remain within their own families, or was it necessary for them to retreat from them? Ways for the Brahma Kumaris to resolve this dilemma were agonised over not only from the inception of the movement but also in Kashmir.

Another cause for reflection was on the role of the *satsang*. While Om Baba and his family were at the Kashmir retreat could the *satsang* survive and grow on its own? How would the new women with leadership potential rise to the challenge? Would the *satsang* evolve new procedures of its own in Hyderabad? Would contact by post be sufficient between Kashmir and Hyderabad? The situation provided not only opportunities but also reasons for some anxiety.

The *Satsang* Continues

During their leader's absence, the members of the *satsang* went on meeting. Indeed during this period the *satsang* flourished and more regular gatherings were organised. The fact that Om Baba was in Kashmir helped this to happen. Daily he wrote letters to Hyderabad which contained elements of wisdom or knowledge, and this routine became the basis of the murlis (messages) that were read out daily at Brahma Kumari centres and that are still read today. In addition poems were also sent. *Murli* is a Hindu word meaning 'flute', and it was taken to refer to Krishna's flute. It was not clear whether the murlis were a product of Om Baba's conscious mind or unconscious one, whether they were revealed by God, or perhaps a combination of different things. In any case, they were taken to be given by God, whether directly or indirectly.

Back in Hyderabad a structured programme began to emerge. Each day would usually begin with a song or poem, and after that the murli from Kashmir would be read out. Beginning sometimes with remarks about the *Bhagavad Gītā*, the murli ranged far and wide over the body of knowledge that was now being built up in the *satsang*. Afterwards, the murli would be commented on, often in the style of a short lecture, by one of the women — Om Radhe and others — who had emerged as leaders. These women, who had not often spoken in public before, found themselves able to discourse in a way that was helpful to their listeners on the topics dealt with by the murlis — the nervous became more confident, the tongue-tied more fluent, the reticent more assertive, the passive more active, and the supposedly weaker sex more strong. The pattern was being set for the future.

Along with the murli and other elements, there was also the practice of meditation. Furthermore, the spiritual experiences known when Om Baba had been present were repeated in his absence. Informants tell of sensations of leaving the body and flying to the soul-world, of feeling light and full of might, of living in a golden-age world, of dancing with Krishna and of feeling bliss. Alongside these extraordinary sensations there were also the more ongoing experiences of being with God and being in the presence of God. What was obvious was that the classes held at Om Niwas were not akin to school classes where one sat and listened to lessons; they were experiential realities for those who attended.

Om Baba's Return to Hyderabad

When Om Baba returned from Kashmir to Hyderabad after months away he found that the *satsang* had attracted new people into its fellowship. His time of retreat had therefore been helpful not only to himself and his family but also to the movement as a whole.

During 1937 the evolving pattern continued of a daily *satsang* involving a song/poem, a murli and meditation. Om Baba remained a charismatic leader, relaying daily messages that added to the store of knowledge of the community. By his own gaze (*drishti*), and by his own spiritual light and might, his very presence was important. Singing and the composition of songs by Om Radhe and others remained significant. Visions too were frequent. As Chander puts it:

> It was also said in Hyderabad that those who came to this *satsang* received self-realisation without making any effort, and that visions were bestowed by God on everyone who came there. So people were naturally attracted there and the number who attended dramatically increased (Chander, 1983b, p. 68).

The numbers included children. Dadi Gulzar, the later head of the Brahma Kumari centre in Delhi and the main trance medium after Om Baba's death, was nine years old at the time. She relates how she went, with her mother, to a series of meetings involving music, dancing and talks. On one occasion, while she was at the *satsang*, she went into a sudden trance in which she found herself drawn into a new inner world rather like Alice in Wonderland's. The wonderland in question was a large bejewelled room with glimmering chandeliers. Through the windows she could see flowing water and idyllic natural scenes featuring gardens and beautiful bushes. In the room itself she saw a handsome ten-year-old prince who beckoned to her to go and play with him. By virtue of the fact that he held a flute in his hand, the adults present deduced from her description that she had seen a vision of Krishna. Other children too claimed to have trance experiences.

The New Spiritual Institution is Founded

By early 1937 the *satsang* and its offshoots in other houses were becoming a kind of pressure cooker of spiritual experience, and it was obvious that the charismatic state of affairs could not continue indefinitely. Something had to be done. There is evidence that although Om Baba did not oppose the visions and trances that were taking place, his concern was beginning to move also towards spiritual education, high values, a more mature and deeply rooted spirituality, and practical matters such as diet and celibacy.

The crux of the matter was that the spiritual movement needed to be properly organised, to prevent it evaporating and dying. Every day as many as a hundred people were congregating in Om Baba's home or one or two other places. Many of them were women and some of them, though young, had assumed positions of 'authority'. The fact that it was mainly women who came was not in itself a problem. They had more free time during the day, many of their men-folk were away, and classically in India women have been attracted into the orbit of ***swamis*** and charismatic religious leaders. What was of concern was the regularity of the meetings — they were held not every week but every day. The growing number attending was also a matter for anxiety. A critical mass was reached when numbers reached fifty, a hundred, and more. Space was disappearing in the bungalows. The level of knowledge and experience of those attending became disparate. Older members such as Om Radhe were receiving the same instruction as any first-day attender. The need for separate groups was beginning to emerge.

There was also the question of what to do with the money that had been accumulated from the sale of Om Baba's jewellery business. Could that be used to found a new institution, and if so what kind would it be? Who would lead it? What was to be done about the incipient opposition that was forming and the wider concern about this extraordinary new development in Hyderabad?

In October 1937 action was therefore taken to ensure a permanent future for the work that had begun at Om Niwas. The nickname of the *satsang* had become Om Mandli (the gathering where 'Om' is chanted). In order to run the community of Om Mandli on an official and legal basis, a management committee was formed, of eleven women. The new institution was to be funded by Om Baba's own money and by his property, which he would transfer to it. This promise of solid financial backing came to legal fruition on 17 February 1938 in a trust deed made by Om Baba. The new trust, the new Om High School and the later university, which was called Prajapita Brahma Kumaris Ishwariya Vishwa Vidyalaya or the Brahma Kumaris World Spiritual University (BKWSU), were institutional matrixes for the growth and spread of the spiritual family.

The formal incorporation of the *satsang* was a momentous development. Women were to be its leaders officially as well as informally. This was remarkable in the India of 1937–8. Three of the eleven women involved as trustees in the will would be of outstanding importance: Om Radhe; Mrs Gopi H. Hathiramani, known as Sister Manmohini, who was a later leader of the community; and Miss Rami G. Hathiramani, known as Dadi Prakashmani, who later still became a key female leader of the community.

Why were women appointed leaders of the new spiritual institution? The Brahma Kumaris say that it was by God's direction, yet other factors could also have come into play here. The first was social. The unfairness of the position of women in Sindi society, and the need for them to be given greater opportunities of service and leadership, had been apparent to Om Baba before the visions began. Here was a chance to use his money, as he would have put it 'under God', to ameliorate the position of women in this new movement. The second reason was a practical one. The natural leaders of the *satsang*, before and after the Kashmir retreat, had been women. Most men were absent or unavailable. In other milieux this would not have been crucial — men would have been appointed anyway — yet to Om Baba it seemed a convincing pragmatic reason why women should run the movement. A third and more metaphysical factor had to do with the sense that a climactic time was at hand. The ages of the world had run their course and a cataclysm was about to occur. During the last two ages (***yugas***) men had been vested with power and authority. At this confluence age, when the old world was passing away and a new world was on the horizon, it was time to redress the balance. In this movement, within the Om Mandli community, women would have the chance to exercise a different kind of leadership. It was now their turn.

In practice, Om Baba remained the effective spiritual leader of the community, but he was able to concentrate more on spirituality and what he considered to be his primary role as God's medium. The day-to-day running of the community passed into the hands of Om Radhe, who was to remain a leading force until her death in 1965. From the Brahma

Kumari perspective however there was just one leader of the community, God Himself, and under Him a man and woman worked together complementing one another.

The Rise of Opposition

In the nature of things it was likely that there would be opposition to what was sometimes conceived to be 'Dada Lekhraj's movement'. The founding of Om Mandli on a more formal basis made it more likely that opposition would harden.

The Hindu tradition has generally been a tolerant one, and in theory it was possible that the new movement would settle down as another Hindu sect (***sampradaya***) and continue as part of the rich Hindu variety. However aspects of the new movement aroused suspicion among Hindus in Hyderabad. According to the *Illustrated Weekly of India* of 13 July 1938:

> Thousands of people in various parts of India who have read more or less garbled accounts of sensational happenings in Hyderabad (Sind) are asking themselves what is this Om Mandli? Is it a new cult of self-restraint and 'self-realisation' with Mr Lekhraj Khubchand as a genuine 'Seeker after the truth'? If not, what was it?

From 1938 to 1939 things did not proceed smoothly for the fledgling community. Opposition to Om Mandli, which eventually turned into a virtual persecution of the Brahma Kumaris, centred round three factors: the rapidity and unexpectedness of its appearance; tension with the Hindu community; and the threats posed by women leaders and celibacy.

The sheer novelty of the phenomenon was a sufficient problem in itself, and as with all new religious movements misunderstandings were rife. The bewildering and rapid change in Om Baba was puzzling even to disinterested onlookers. He seemed too old. His past life as diamond merchant, pillar of the community, and a pious and rich Hindu had given no clue to what was happening now. In the 13 July 1938 *Illustrated Weekly of India* article mentioned above the reporter also comments:

> In appearance Mr Lekhraj is elderly though well preserved, and his features have the stamp not only of the ascetic but also of the intellectual. We can easily discount therefore the stories attributing a misuse of hypnotic powers over neurotic young women.

News however percolated out alluding to Om Baba and his women followers as 'Krishna and his *gopīs* (cowgirls)', and this illustrated the possibility of misunderstanding, whether it was malicious or accidental. Sexual adventurism by Om Baba was, of course, the opposite of the truth.

A second general reason for opposition to the group which was to become the Brahma Kumaris was their ambivalent relationship to the Hindu community. They used the same Hindu words such as Shiva, Brahma and Vishnu, and they read Hindu texts such as the *Bhagavad Gītā*, because Om Baba had adapted Hindu ideas from his own Hindu Sindi tradition. This incurred a certain amount of incomprehension and suspicion on the part of the Hindu community, and was comparable by analogy to the more violent reaction of the Shi'ite Muslim community in Iran to the rise of the Baha'is in the mid-nineteenth century. One example of Om Baba's nearness to Hindu thought while deviating from it lies in his attitude to the end of the world and the coming of a new golden age. The classical Hindu tradition held to the notion of history as a cycle of four ages (*yugas*), which are in decline from the golden age and the silver age through to the copper age and the iron age (*kali yuga*) where we are now. Om Baba accepted this viewpoint. Classical Hindu belief was that the present, weakest *kali yuga* would end and there would be a new golden age. Om Baba agreed with this too. The difference lay in the way that Om Baba speeded up the whole process and made it more dramatic and immediate. His thought was still developing in 1937–8, and he was beginning to believe that the classical Hindi view of the *yugas* made them unimaginably long and virtually meaningless. In about 1942 he finally abandoned the classical view of the *yugas* lasting for millions of years and fixed on the notion of a cycle of history of 5,000 years. He felt that the world as we know it would disappear in a series of disasters involving natural calamities, civil wars and a final cataclysm. However another golden age would follow almost immediately. It would be a paradise on earth involving a population that was small, and there would be natural beauty in abundance. It would be a time of peace and harmony, painless birth and death, fine relationships and equality between the sexes. The imminence of the end of the present world and the rise of the golden age gave a great urgency to contemporary life. It was possible to anticipate this new scenario, to make appropriate spiritual preparations for it and to gain a place in the body of people who would be alive on this earth during the golden age.

Elsewhere in India in 1937 Sri Aurobindo was also prophesying about a kind of golden age to come on earth. But in his thought the golden age would evolve creatively out of the world process. It would not, as in Om Baba's thought, follow after a calamitous collapse. And in any case Sri Aurobindo's views were almost as distant from classical Hindu thought as Om Baba's (Whaling, 1979).

To a number of Hindus, even if they were unsophisticated, Om Baba's views were unusual. Millenarianism might be alright for Christians with their notion of the Second Coming of Christ, for Jews with their belief in the coming of the Messiah, for Muslims with their expectation of the Mahdi's arrival, and even for Buddhists with their notion of the coming of Maitreya Buddha, but it was not appropriate for Hindus.

The reasons described above for opposition to the work of Om Baba might not have been conclusive without the third — Om Baba's stress on celibacy (***brahmacharya***), even in marriage, and his emphasis on the leadership of women. This seemed to be threaten the established order in society, both social and religious. After all, Sindi society was run by men in all its sectors — family, community and religious matters. Furthermore, sex was an important element in family life, and it was an activity governed mainly by men. On return from their travels Hyderabad merchants were not best pleased to learn that their women-folk were reluctant to grant sexual favours after joining Om Baba's movement. Suspicion was heightened by the institutionalisation of Om Mandli as a trust led by women. Moreover the departure of Nirmal Shanta from her husband's and father-in-law's home was another straw in the wind of discontent. Meanwhile celibacy held echoes of virtue for the Hindu psyche, and Mahatma Gandhi was extolling its merits elsewhere in India. However the Om Mandli view of celibacy seemed to be a kind of unprecedented unilateral declaration of independence.

Thus, while the Sindi Hindus might theoretically have seen Om Mandli as a new and unusual *sampradaya*, it did not quite work out that way, and from 1937 to 1939 was a time of testing and opposition for the institution that evolved out of the *satsang* at Om Niwas.

The Opening of Om High School

As family groups were becoming associated with the *satsang*, it became necessary to provide for the needs of children so, Om Baba envisaged a special kind of high school. In embryo he was imagining the Brahma Kumari World Spiritual University that would later come into being. The immediate requirement was for a high school for youngsters to supplement the daily classes for adults that were already taking place. Thus a boarding school for children named Om High School was opened in 1937 in Om Baba's own large home, part of which was adapted for the purpose. It was to provide a complete education founded on high principles of spirituality. The long-term implicit aim would be to create a body of people who would be motivated to pass on to others the gifts of peace of mind, purity of life and other ideal qualities that would lead into a new age.

A basic education was given in reading, writing and arithmetic. A spiritual education and practical arts were taught as well. The older women in the movement and the younger gifted women were involved in the work of the school, and there were classes for boys as well as girls.

The schedule for a typical day would start when the children rose at 5am and had light exercise and a walk followed by a meditation on peace. At 6.30 they had a bath and ate breakfast, and at 8am their studies began. A recess came at 10.30, when they were given a fruit snack, then classes continued from 11am to 1pm. After lunch and a siesta, at 3pm there were classes in spiritual knowledge then songs and conversations. A 5pm drink of milk was followed by an evening walk. Dinner was at 7.30pm and from 8.30 to 10pm there were informal talks and counselling about how to attain the best qualities in oneself, the importance of pure diet, how to handle the dilemmas of everyday life, and other points of knowledge raised by the children. After some meditation, at 10pm it was time to go to sleep. Seven hours remained for that until 5am the next day.

In the life of the school, physical recreation and play were catered for. The children were taught to do their own housework as a form of *karma* yoga (the yoga of work). This was a new experience for those whose families had had servants. The spiritual knowledge communicated in the *satsangs* through the daily murlis was given to them as well, so pupils received an all-round education involving body, mind and spirit. However the teachers were not professionally trained, and the school had not been recognised by the government.

Rumours soon arose about what was, or what might be, going on at Om High School. Yet when local educational administrators arrived at the school unannounced to conduct surprise visits of inspection they were impressed by the atmosphere, by the demeanour of the students, by their rapport with each other, by their devotion to study and by their apparent maturity beyond their years. The inspectors' concern was not with the school itself, where they were welcomed and it was clear there was nothing to hide. Their unease was about the long-term future of the school. Would it last, and how would it fare financially without government support?

Om Radhe's response was that God would provide. However their doubts about the future of the school in Hyderabad had some validity. Indeed the future of the total community in Hyderabad was being thrown into increasing jeopardy.

Growing Opposition

At the end of 1937 and the beginning of 1938 opposition to the *satsang*, the trust and Om High School increased further — the issue of immediate concern being that of celibacy. If girls or widows joined the *satsang*, or if boys or widowers became involved, there was no insuperable problem. The real difficulty occurred with married women, and less often married men. If the partner agreed to live a celibate marriage all would be well. If however the partner did not want to do so there was a real dilemma — and it was not only a personal one but also a social one with repercussions in the community.

In the mind of Om Baba celibacy was bound up with the need for each person to be a pure soul in the extraordinary confluence age that had dawned. It was important to get rid of body-consciousness and be imbued with soul-consciousness, and — based on his visions — Om Baba interpreted sex as part of body-consciousness. To be serious about the spiritual life meant total commitment to God, to soul-consciousness and to effort on behalf of the world. Such seriousness was incompatible with sexual activity.

Om Baba's rationale for celibacy was not unlike that for becoming a nun or a monk. Indeed the *satsang* women were popularly known as nuns or ***gopis*** (milkmaids associated with Krishna). The call to a spiritual life was paramount. Nevertheless, Om Baba's critique went deeper than this. After all, the founder of his father's order, the Vallabhacharis, had felt the call to get married for spiritual ends. Moreover the early Christians believed that they were living at the 'end of the age', as Albert Schweitzer (1954) points out in his *Quest of the Historical Jesus*. During that extraordinary end-time marriage was at best a mixed blessing — and yet it was better 'to marry than to burn'. For Om Baba marriage in itself was not wrong. He denounced celibates (*sannyasis*) who left their families to their own devices. It was sex in marriage that was the problem. True spiritual vitality took one beyond sex which was a symbol of ego and of body-consciousness. Sex was also a symbol of the control that men had over women. Sex must be transcended and left behind in the 'crisis age' that had now dawned.

It is not absolutely clear when Om Baba explicitly denounced sex inside as well as outside marriage. *The Illustrated Weekly of India* article of 13 July 1938 leaves the issue somewhat open:

> It may be that the repercussions of his teaching were not of his own seeking nor is evidence really available that he has actually induced married women to renounce their conjugal vows.

Whether his teaching was explicit or not the tenor of Om Baba's views could hardly be mistaken.

In the months before June 1938 matters steadily worsened. An Anti-Om Mandli committee was formed to co-ordinate action against Om Baba. Its main plank of concern was that young women who had opted for celibacy through joining the *satsang* should be allowed to marry, and that married women who had opted for celibacy after joining the movement should be allowed to re-engage in sexual intercourse with their husbands. The committee argued that the tenets of Hindu law and the laws of nature themselves were on their side. Om Baba had to a degree anticipated this by requiring girls and married women who attended the *satsang* to bring written letters of permission from their father or husband. Some were forthcoming; others were not.

Another irritant about the general lifestyle in the Om Mandli community was the denigration of things such as meat, alcohol, costly clothes and material status.

It is possible to see both sides of the dispute. As far as Om Mandli was concerned, they had faith in God and allegiance to what they considered to be true religion, to purity of mind and actions, and to the new knowledge they had imbibed. From Om Baba's viewpoint he was not forcing the women to come to Om Niwas; they came of their own accord. It was not he who was giving the command to celibacy; it was God whose servant he was who advised it in the *Bhagavad Gītā*. In the Brahma Kumari records there are stories of true bravery emanating from that period. Some of the women were abused, some were beaten, some had their possessions confiscated, some were thrown out of the house, others were locked up, and some were forbidden to go near Om Niwas again. Other women were even chained to their beds and deprived of food for days at a time. For wives who had been used to submitting to their husbands or fathers, such steadfastness in defence of their new principles was startling and surprising. They were determined to keep their vows of chastity and celibacy.

From the Anti-Om Mandli committee's viewpoint, marriage included sex. To withdraw sex on a permanent basis was not in accord with the tenets of Hindu *dharma*. Their women had now done this — the point was not in dispute — but while under the influence of the teachings of Om Baba. Therefore his community should be regulated and, if necessary, prohibited. The renunciation of sex by the married women in his *satsang* was unacceptable. Such a radical autonomy, whether justified spiritually or not, was an infringement of natural, religious and community law. Society was not ready for it, so the committee argued.

As the dispute grew, both sides were polarised due to their clash of world-views. Possibly, the ultimate departure of the movement from Hyderabad might have been avoided if such pressures had not built up. Petty insults were combined with matters of principle to make compromise less likely. Some of the local press and some civic leaders turned even more hostile. Om Baba's brother-in-law, the *mukhi*, became more aggressive. Ruffians were hired to harass Om Mandli members. Threats were made of possible excommunication from caste. Money was raised to further the campaign against Om Mandli. Politicians were approached for support.

In the midst of all this hubbub Om Baba kept Om Mandli in operation. He continued to relay the daily murlis to the community, the school remained open, and members of the community held bravely to their principles. Indeed an attempt was made to view the Anti-Om Mandli committee creatively on the principle that one's persecutors can really be one's friends. However by condemning all sex as sex-lust without explanation Om Mandli too was open to misinterpretation. While various sexual demands made by the Hyderabad men may have amounted to selfishness and carnal lust, other sexual overtures did not necessarily fit into this category, and could be more naïve, innocent and open to mutuality. Some of the men knew that their wives still loved them in a spiritual way but not all felt ready to take up a celibate marriage, and they also understood that they were not guilty of lust. There were hurtful and sorrowful misunderstandings. The early Brahma Kumaris, although tolerant and loving in general ways, were not able to compromise on their commitment to celibacy as part of their betrothal to soul-consciousness over body-consciousness. And this poignant dual motive — of wishing to remain in the family and yet to cleave to celibacy and soul-consciousness — has remained a source of ambiguity ever since.

Matters came to a head on 21 June 1938, when some of the aggrieved husbands and their comrades marched on Om Niwas to force a showdown. A confused series of events ensued during which the marchers tried to get inside the building but were bravely and peacefully repulsed by the women. During the melee a fire started, and serious tragedy was averted only by the arrival of responsible officials, a strong police force and the fire brigade.

The Bhaibund ***panchayat*** (community assembly) became involved in the disagreement. Some of the husbands requested early permission to remarry, and the wives were not averse to this because they could see the hardship suffered by their husbands. There are even stories of some young women becoming matchmakers and trying to find suitable wives for their husbands to relieve them of a sexual burden they could no longer carry.

The *panchayat* appointed a special committee under Mr Mangharam to investigate the matter, and evidence was taken from various sides. However interpreted, the facts were not in doubt. Young women and wives, after becoming associated with the *satsang*, had become convinced about the need for celibacy, and would not turn away from their convictions. The committee took quite a hard line and found that the 'women's celibacy movement' was difficult to reconcile with Hindu *dharma* and that restrictions should be placed on the Om Mandli *satsangs* and work.

In Hyderabad there was a partial reaction against the Anti-Om Mandli committee for taking things too far, and a court judgement of 21 November 1938 partly vindicated Om Mandli. However matters had become too serious for the *satsang* to remain in the city in an atmosphere of confusion. Enquiries about property in Karachi were made, and arrangements were put in hand for Om Mandli to move to somewhere that they could continue to work in what was hoped would be an atmosphere of peace and calm.

4

Om Mandli in Karachi

With hindsight, Om Mandli's move to Karachi in 1939 was an excellent decision. The new environment was able to provide the Brahma Kumaris with the opportunity to start again in a new milieu. They needed a time of reflection as well as one of calm, renewal, thought, meditation, fellowship and waiting to find out what future service would entail. Their small campus comprised initially five bungalows; these were named Baby Bhavan, Boys Bhavan, Prem Bhavan, Radha Bhavan and Om Nivas. Gradually, the community began to settle down in this larger city.

Om Baba was not well known in Karachi. However Bhai Lekhraj had some supporters in Karachi, and some people there declared that he was a maligned man whose teachings were those of a saint and that by following his simple way eternal life could be obtained.

For the sake of propriety in Hyderabad Om Mandli, through Om Baba and Om Radhe, required its members to obtain letters of permission from the heads of their households for them to reside on the campus in Karachi. Many of the members, brothers and sisters, received these letters immediately and they joined Om Mandli in its new location. For others there would be a longer wait and greater hardship, but in time most of them were able to transfer from Hyderabad to Karachi.

Throughout most of the time in Karachi well over a hundred people — up to four hundred, at one stage — lived in the community. They came from similar but slightly different social and economic strata, and backgrounds. They began the difficult task of applying in a communal setting what they had learnt in Hyderabad. The difference now was that they were together for the whole time and did not disperse to separate homes after the *satsang*. They learnt to see each other and treat each other as souls who happened to inhabit the bodies of males or females, young or old people. Exclusive attachment to relatives was transcended as the community became a spiritual family whose basic attachment was to Brahma Baba. The assumption was that one's sex was an adventitious thing. Over the span of rebirths one had belonged to both sexes equally. The body was a vehicle of the soul, and as such it was of secondary importance. What mattered was the soul, and to see each other as souls.

A daily programme began not only for the school, which reopened quickly and had a revamped programme, but also for the whole community. An inspiring tune was played both to wake everyone and as a way to fix the mind on God at the start of the day. Sitting in bed the members of the community engaged in meditation, and then did appropriate bodily exercise. At 5.30am the murli was read and reflected on. Then it was time for breakfast, which was followed by daily chores such as laundry, preparing food, doing odd jobs and office work. After lunch — often eaten in silence — there would be a siesta, or conversation with others, or the opportunity to attend to one's own needs. In the late afternoon another group meditation occurred and then dinner was served. After the meal Om Baba and Om Radhe gave classes on various aspects of knowledge; these sometimes took the form of a discursive reflection on the murli that had been read that morning. Quiet meditation prepared the way, through its focus on remembrance of God, for a time of sleep when the mind was likely to rest in unconscious thoughts about the God who had been experienced inwardly last thing at night, and who would be encountered again first thing in the morning. In this way a daily programme, a life regimen, an integrated lifestyle and a communal pattern emerged.

The Last Persecution

Before fuller peace and calm could reign, Om Mandli had to undergo a final trauma at the hands of the Anti-Om Mandli committee. The withdrawal of the community from Hyderabad to Karachi had solved the problem for some of them by the expedient of separation. For others the break had not been made as some women had been forbidden to leave Hyderabad. These women received letters from Om Baba, and they also met from time to time. Eventually fifteen of them took matters into their own hands and travelled to Karachi. Naively they wrote back to Hyderabad to report that they had arrived safely in Karachi and all was well.

Their departure was a blow to the vanity of the families concerned as these women had left without permission. Moreover asking their families not to worry was not likely to reduce their anxiety. The old misunderstandings resurfaced. The families of the women who had fled now or before met representatives of the Anti-Om Mandli committee. They decided to give financial support to a major lawsuit that was coming to trial in Hyderabad — it involved a husband who was suing for the restitution of conjugal rights. A gifted lawyer was hired with the aim of ridiculing Om Radhe in the witness box because, as they rightly surmised, she was young and inexperienced and not accustomed to public speaking outside the confines of the *satsang*. In the event the ploy misfired. Om Radhe defended her position well and in an unorthodox manner. When asked to take an oath on the *Bhagavad Gītā* in the presence of God she refused to do so but affirmed that God is omnipresent. When asked why the women had run away, she said:

> Judge Saheb, have you ever read the Shrimat Bhagvat scripture (the ***Bhāgavata Purāna***)? When the Lord (Krishna) played His flute, why did the *gopis* (cowgirls) run to Him intoxicated? Why were not cases filed against them in court? The flute referred to in the scripture is actually the flute of which we are hearing through the mouth of Dada. It is the incomparable knowledge of God.
>
> Let me ask you, Judge Saheb, if a man leaves his family and takes *sannyas* (religious vows) why is no legal case ever filed against him? In the eyes of God, men and women are equal. Now God has put the urn of Knowledge on the heads of women. So when we mothers have the opportunity of attaining purity and wisdom, naturally we cannot refuse. Why does not everyone rejoice over such newfound purity and elevation? Why are these questions put to us? The answer is clear, Judge Saheb. Whatever difficulties have been put in our path, whatever hardships and abuses have been inflicted on us by our own relatives and friends, are all a reaction to our purity (Chander, 1983b, p. 133).

Om Radhe's spirited defence has gone down in Brahma Kumari folklore as being comparable to the court scene in the great Hindu Epic, the ***Mahābhārata***, in which Draupadi found that her sari and her honour were being continually being replenished by God when her sari was being stripped from her. The Judge had never come across a situation like it. In answer to one of his final questions about how many children Om Baba had, she replied that Om Mandli did not look to Om Baba but to the Supreme Soul who happened to have come down in his body. The question then was how many children did God have? 'All souls are His children', she said, 'not only am I or those who attend this *satsang* His children, but you, Sir, are also His child' (Chander, 1983b, p. 134).

Part of the beneficial outcome from Om Radhe's witness testimony at the trial, and the surrounding events, was that it became clear to both sides that the Om Mandli women were sincere and meant what they said, even though their beliefs might not stand four-square with established social opinion of the day. Previously, the Anti-Om Mandli committee of 1938–9 had viewed 'cult members' as passive victims of recruitment methods that brainwashed and hypnotised people into passive obedience. The same incomprehension for the real motives of family members joining a new movement, the same regard for family honour and the same sense that family members were being manipulated and controlled appeared in the anti-cult movements from the 1970s in the West, of which the Anti-Om Mandli committee was a forerunner.

Some of the women were taken back by their families to Hyderabad, but they stuck to their principles. They avoided meat, wore simple white clothes, eschewed expensive entertainments and did not accept marriage although they did the housework. They continued their practice of meditation and remained in remembrance of the presence of God. Finally, their families realised that they were steadfast and sincere, and that they wished to return to Karachi, so permission was given. Tickets were bought, and the women went to join Om Baba and the community.

Although the battle to establish the integrity and autonomy of the new movement in Karachi was won, paradoxically two of the most disturbing outward incidents in the saga still remained to be played out. In spite of a speech by the Chief Minister of Sind in the Sind Parliament on 26 March 1939 defending Om Mandli on the grounds of religious freedom, the coalition government appointed a tribunal to consider a prohibiting order against Om Mandli. Somewhat inevitably, the *ex parte* tribunal recommended that the members of Om Mandli should not be allowed to remain together. However some members of the public in Karachi objected to what they saw as the hounding of the community, and the Chief Minister made it known that if the Brahma Kumaris kept a low profile they would be left in peace.

In a final desperate gesture, the Anti-Om Mandli committee is alleged to have hired a Sikh to harm Om Baba in Karachi. When he gained access to the presence of the one who had been described to him as Om Baba the Sikh could not go through with the intention to harm him. He found himself internally overwhelmed by the spiritual presence of Om Baba and allowed himself to be apprehended. He was treated well and allowed to leave. From then on the fellowship was left in peace.

The recent past had been a disturbing time for both sides. The depth of ill-feeling towards a former colleague, which had led to an attempt to harm him, is evidence of the passions aroused. Reminiscences of Dadi Chandramani, a later co-leader of the Brahma Kumaris, who as a teenager was dubbed by Om Baba as the 'lioness of the Punjab', attest to the bravery and determination of the members of the community to hold fast at a demanding time.

The underlying hope of the Anti-Om Mandli committee had been that the movement would founder and disintegrate, once the members would come to realise that their experiences had amounted to delusion. The euphoria would disappear and they would quarrel and disagree, and would eventually return home. Their spiritual fervour would disintegrate when they were faced with the daily realities of living together. Once the committee realised that the movement was 'for real' Om Mandli was left in peace.

A Separated Community in Karachi and Its World-view

The Brahma Kumaris community in the outskirts of Karachi largely cut itself off from the surrounding world except for contact with local people for food, produce, services and other necessary items. The members had their own priorities, and for eleven years they were able to develop and deepen their lives within the parameters of an independent campus virtually immune to the wider life that was oscillating around them, although there was an awareness of the outbreak and escalation of the Second World War. How then did their lives and world-view develop?

Fascinating evidence is present in a booklet (Om Rādhe, 1943) dated August 1943 unearthed in the Bodleian Library in Oxford. It is one of the few written records available from that period, as the original murlis from the early years have either disappeared or cannot be dated accurately. It appears that the booklet was one of a number sent round the world at that time. It intimates that such letters in various languages had occasionally been sent by registered post to all prominent people in the public eye such as His Majesty the King, Her Majesty the Queen, Her Royal Highness Princess Elizabeth, ministers, viceroys, governors, rajas, ranis and all other well-known religious and political leaders. It states that sending the free booklet was considered a divine duty performed by the Brahma Kumaris age after age in order to let people know about themselves and their work. Whether King George VI or the other dignitaries mentioned actually read the booklet is doubtful. However the decision to send this literature to influential people was important.

Om Radhe signed the letter accompanying the booklet, and she apparently had a similar intention in mind to that of Baha'ullah, the effective founder of the Baha'i tradition, who also wrote, from his situation of exile at the end of the nineteenth century, to various contemporary monarchs, including Queen Victoria, in order to inform them about an important new phenomenon. The extraordinary thing is that, from a position of exile in the case of Baha'ullah and from a small presence in a tiny compound in Karachi in the case of the Brahma Kumaris, there was an ability to foresee an international future from a situation of straightened circumstances.

Initial Strategy in Karachi

At first however there had been no wish to interact with the wider world by for example sending letters to world leaders, in spite of the notions that all humans were seen as souls and that the small Karachi family could become a world family. The initial period was a time for inward renewal, for building up the immediate community, and for strengthening and developing core doctrines and spiritualities in the hope that in the long run — if there was a long run — the time would come for expansion and a wider vision.

What the Buddha would have called 'skill in means' was lacking in this early period when the community was cut off, the vilification of the pioneers was still real, the newness of the message was vibrant yet incomplete, and the end of the world in its present form seemed imminent. Presentation of the core world-view would later be refined in the light of growth, a greater sensitivity towards and contact with the wider world, and a realisation of the need to communicate more empathetically with people who could not be expected to accept a startlingly new message on a take-it-or-leave-it basis.

It is worth pausing for a moment to summarise the world-view being enunciated by Om Baba as the movement that had started around him now settled in Karachi. His viewpoint centred on his vision of God as the Supreme Soul who was a personal force of light, bliss and peace communicating with him from the soul-world that was separate from this material world. Om Baba had formed the conviction that God, the Supreme Soul, had been inactive in the soul-world for almost 5,000 years but had now become active through Om Baba himself as a channel. This was a climactic time in the history of the world. The last degenerate age of *kali yuga* was due to culminate in a series of catastrophes which from another point-of-view would be a blessing in disguise. It would be a time of transformation, so it would herald radical change and the almost immediate reappearance of a new golden age on earth. During this intermediate period, when the old world of *kali yuga* was passing away and the new golden age was struggling to appear, God would be supremely active and available to people in the world. The present confluence age linking the old world to the new one was an unparalleled time of spiritual potential and power. It was up to the world to use this important and spiritually vibrant time to the full, and the Brahma Kumaris were the heralds of this new dispensation.

Om Baba's visions of the end of the present age in a welter of explosions and natural disasters (later interpreted as a nuclear holocaust), and of the golden age to follow, were new eastern variations of an apocalyptic vision. The world in its present phase would end but not in an absolute sense. During this confluence age, Om Baba suggested, it was necessary to live humbly and yet triumphantly as anticipatory apostles of a new golden age of ecological beauty and spiritual power. In order to be effective it was necessary to retreat from 'body-consciousness' and live in 'soul-consciousness'. Overcoming body-consciousness did not involve retreating literally from the world to live the solitary life of a holy person (*sannyasi*), nor did it mean neglecting the body as such, which still required disciplined washing, holistic health care, satisfying vegetarian food and sufficient rest. However it did include abstinence from selfishness, from distracting worldly pursuits, from absorption in material matters and from indulgence in sex. Creatively it entailed the development of a deep spirituality centred on the notion that each person is essentially not a 'body' but a 'soul'. Outward bodily and worldly features of sex, race, colour, attractiveness, nationality or dress were superficial and of quite secondary importance. It was important to treat each person as a soul requiring tolerance, calmness, love, generosity and civility, and thus to make them vessels of peace and the like.

Underlying all this was the need for a deep and genuine spirituality which was now eminently possible because God Himself was immediately available to those willing to accept the love and peace He was willing to give. The spiritual power emanating from God was sufficient to satisfy the deepest spiritual aspirations of each soul, to make them instruments of peace, and possibly, if time allowed, to send them out in service to the rest of the world.

This was the framework of knowledge imparted through the murlis, in talks and in other ways, by Om Baba to those who had been and were with him at this period. Although this knowledge would grow and evolve tremendously, the core world-view remains roughly similar right up to this day.

Personal Disappointment and Later Growth

In Karachi there was an interesting combination of feeling that members were participating in a drama that was a repetition of what had happened 5,000 years ago and therefore could be seen in a detached way, while at the same time the participants were dissatisfied personally at what had happened to the new community. The disappointment took three forms: these related to Om Baba himself; to the community's dismay at the treatment of women; and to their sorrow in relation to their Hindu neighbours and those from other religious traditions.

Om Baba felt that those among whom he had been born had failed to recognise him. They considered him to be a person of no consequence, and even as an abductor of virgins and others. He knew however that this would be temporary, and that it would in time be subsumed into a wider perspective. However it rankled initially.

Meanwhile Om Radhe felt that women had been downgraded and degraded, and treated as 'innocent little turtles' who could be maltreated. She and the women objected to this, and a sense of betrayal remained overt during the early Karachi period. Later, once the trauma could be recollected in tranquillity and in the light of the cycle, some of the families and other people involved in the Anti-Om Mandli affair were reconciled.

Likewise, there was a sense of disappointment in relation to other religions, which were viewed as no religions in the true sense of the word. The early Brahma Kumaris were also disillusioned after their experiential contact, especially with Krishna and the *Bhagavad Gītā*, and the more popular elements in the Hindu tradition. According to Om Baba the *Bhagavad Gītā* was the crown jewel of all world scriptures, but it had been misinterpreted by Hindus and by their superstitious devotion (***bhakti***) at local level.

Persecution and their intense spiritual experience combined to give the Brahma Kumaris a confidence out of all proportion to their numbers, an exclusivity based on revelatory conviction rather than a sensitive awareness of others, and a determination that would enable them to forge a new religious/spiritual movement of potentially deep significance.

The 'souls' in Karachi saw themselves as Brahmins, even though a number of them were members of the **Vaishya** (the third Hindu caste) by birth. This caused more friction with the Hindus, who considered that it was only feasible to be born a Brahmin (the first Hindu caste by birth) as this was a matter of genes and heredity. Meanwhile the Brahma Kumaris maintained that all people in the present iron age, whatever their caste birth, were actually **Shudras** (fourth Hindu caste). Only when one became God's child, when one became twice-born, when one became a 'Brahmin of the mouth-born dynasty of Brahma' (a Brahma Kumari), did one attain the status of Brahmin in the confluence age that was now present on earth.

Community Arrangements in Karachi

The original five bungalows in the Karachi community were renamed and gradually increased to eight, and living quarters were set up for different kinds of 'souls': for families; men; women; mothers and babies; boys; and girls. The central meeting point was established at King Bhavan, and three bungalows were occupied in the Clifton Beach area (later to be taken over by the Russian Embassy in Pakistan). Om Baba lived in the Kripalani bungalow, which became known as Baba Bhavan, where he was not in constant contact with his people — unlike in Hyderabad and later Mount Abu. The Clifton bungalows were two miles away from Baba Bhavan. Also at a distance was the Gulzar Bhavan for mothers and babies, the Sadar Bazar Bhavan for families and the Soldier Bazar Bhavan for boys. At another place, known as Killarney bungalow, Sister Manmohini, who was later prominent in the movement, opened a tailoring shop. Separate facilities were established for a laundry, kitchens, office work, car repairs, carpentry, tailoring, work on books, and so on.

Because Om Baba had separate living quarters, the arrangements for the murlis were more flexible. He could write them singly or in batches in his own bungalow, and they could be read out by Om Radhe or one of the other women. It was possible to transport everyone to one of the bungalows, usually King Bhavan, where this could be done. There might also be lectures separate from the murlis, as well as commentaries on the murlis, which could be given at different times, for example in the evening. Another evening feature, including the children, was a time of self-examination, when members could be honest about their shortcomings and get help with them.

A Millennial Sense

During the early years of the Karachi community there was a certain millennial sense among the members due in part to the Second World War, which was deemed to be a rerun of the Mahābhārata War of 5,000 years earlier, as mentioned in the *Mahābhārata* epic. This is brought out in the 1943 Bodleian booklet (Om Rādhe, 1943) whose full title was *The Preordained World-wide War of Mahabarata and its Result*.

Om Baba speeded up the Hindu view of the cycles and made it more specific. He was already thinking in terms of a total cycle of 5,000 years divided into 1,250 years each. These four ages would constitute the golden, silver, copper and iron ages. At the end of the fourth age there would be a time of confluence, bridging the end of the iron age, and the start of a new golden age that would follow almost immediately. The end of the iron age (*kali yuga*) would be marked by a great war. He identified this with the war featured in the *Mahābhārata*. One traditional date for the Mahābhārata War was 3102 BCE, and it was possible to see the date of 1943 as being roughly the end-point of the whole cycle. In any event, the whole thought process brought a sense of impending doom-cum-transformation as being relevant and not impossible.

Although Om Baba's view was close in some respects to the apocalyptic notion of the end to be found in Christian theories of the Second Coming of Christ, Jewish theories of the Messiah, and Shi'ite Islamic theories of the Mahdi, it also picked up echoes in Hindu thought. The end of the world, for Om Baba, was not absolute — it was the end of the present cycle — and all the cycles and the confluence age were repetitions of what had gone before.

In the Bodleian booklet (Om Rādhe, 1943) there are some uncompromising apocalyptic passages that are in striking contrast to the more mellow nature of recent Brahma Kumari thought. It is interesting to note that the same switch from apocalyptic fire to irenicism occurs within the Baha'i tradition. The forerunner of Baha'ullah, the Bab, had offered a sterner message from 1844 to 1850 until he was put to death by the Persian state. Baha'ullah, his successor and effective founder of the Baha'i tradition, modified the message in order to take it in a more peaceful direction, and it was his interpretation that prevailed (Momen, 2006, pp. 138–42).

The thrust of the millenarian situation of the early Brahma Kumaris turned them inwards to ponder as a family the meaning of their destiny and to prepare earnestly for whatever future might lie ahead. The outline of the future they basically knew — it was the actual dynamics and 'when' of that future that were not yet so certain.

Later Developments in Karachi

After the end of the Second World War in 1945, Om Mandli started to relate more to the outside world. For example, the murlis began to be delivered in Hindi even though the early Brahma Kumaris were almost totally Sindi by birth and language. The reason must surely have been that Hindi is the dominant language in north India, and was to become the national language of India, whereas Sindi catered for only a minority of Indians.

In addition to the free booklet (Om Rādhe, 1943) distributed during the Second World War, letters were later sent to other people in wider India and in different parts of the world. Letters, telegrams or murlis, for example, were addressed to Gandhi, Raja Gopalacharya (president of the All-India Women's Association), religious leaders at a conference in Colombo, the kings of Jamnagar, Jodhpur and Mandavi, the governor of Sind, the mayor of Karachi, and (on 2 May 1947) to King George VI, as well as President

Truman. One wonders what King George VI made of the opening paragraph of his letter:

> Dear soul in the form of King George. This world is an endless drama which repeats every 5,000 years. You are an actor in this great drama. Do you know that 5,000 years ago you acted the same role as the King of England, in this same body at the same time and with the same name? And that you will act the same role again after 5,000 years (Chander, 1983b, pp. 207–8).

The level of sophistication is not the point. It is the desire to make deeper contact with the wider world that is important.

Another change was that newcomers who were not from Sind, especially Gujaratis, were finding their way in small numbers into the Brahma Kumari community. The long-term inference here was that the Brahma Kumaris were not a clique of Sindis but a movement of more widespread interest.

Om Baba received a message from God that the Brahma Kumaris were now more mature and filled with godly power, and it was time to reconnect with the parents and relatives of the community, and to all those who had harmed them, after six or seven years of separation. The aim was not only humanitarian but also a means of outreach. Six conditions were laid down: to remain in soul-consciousness, to refuse money, to eat vegetarian food, to avoid hugs, to give the relatives 'supreme knowledge' and to operate with bliss and power. This was as it were a trial run and a harbinger of the future world service.

Another important change of emphasis after 1945 was that Om Mandli adopted the name by which it is now known — Brahma Kumaris. Brahma Baba was now also known as Prajapita Brahma Baba, and the university would be called by his name. In a picture of the cycle dated 1949, the address is: Prajapiti Brahma Kumaris, Avinashi Gyan Yagya (Om Mandli), Bleakhouse Road, P. O. Box 381, Karachi, (Pak).

The Role of Pictures

Om Mandli also decided to introduce pictures for internal use as well as when broadcasting the murli to a wider world. These would later be used in Brahma Kumari centres and meeting places around the world. The main pictures focused on Brahma Baba (as Om Baba was now known), Om Radhe (as Mama), the golden age to come, Shiva Baba (God) in an egg-shaped form circled by light, the cycle of world history, the cosmic tree (world history in another form) and the three worlds (matter, the subtle region and the soul-world).

Although some elements of these pictures were received through trance visions, trance experiences were now becoming less common. Brahma Baba's visions and the trances of others, which had been vital at the beginning of the movement, had been partly triggered by the chanting of OM, and the rise of the *satsang* had coincided with numerous people enjoying rich experiences. There had been a sense of 'spiritual magic'. However this was being replaced by a deeper understanding and a developing wisdom, and trances by the mid-1940s were less common. Brahma Baba, Dadi Gulzar (who became the trance medium of the movement) and a few others still experienced trances, which provided new knowledge. However a trance as a fun or pleasure thing became less important. Study, knowledge, meditation and a deepening spirituality were seen as the keys, and although trances remained they were no longer strenuously sought.

The position of other religious traditions was now re-examined and respected more, partly influenced by the importance of producing pictures. How would they be fitted into the cycle of world history picture, or the cosmic tree picture, when they were elaborated and drawn in picture form? Other possibilities began to open up, and dialogue about the role of other religions became possible.

Pictures that represented new developments in Brahma Kumari life and thought were deemed especially important. Increasingly the pictures painted in this Karachi period, and later, became not merely internal creations but also methods of forging links with the outside world. They would later be used as instruments in an innovative Indian form of evangelism.

Three Worlds

In their view of life so far there had been a knowledge of two worlds: the physical, material, bodily world in which souls know themselves to be living; and the soul-world, where the Supreme Soul 'God' — called 'Shiva Baba' by Brahma Baba — dwells completely separate from the material world. It is a silent world and is the ultimate home of human souls, and it is here that they stay in silence before being born into the physical world and after returning from the physical world. No direct contact is possible between the soul-world and the world of matter. The Supreme Soul, Shiva Baba, is not present nor could He be present in this physical world. He is therefore not omnipresent.

In the current confluence age, the soul-world had become available to human beings because the Supreme Soul had come to earth in the body of Brahma Baba. Through Brahma Baba the Supreme Soul could be made available on earth, and human beings, when they woke up to the fact that

4.1: The Three Worlds – physical, angelic and soul.

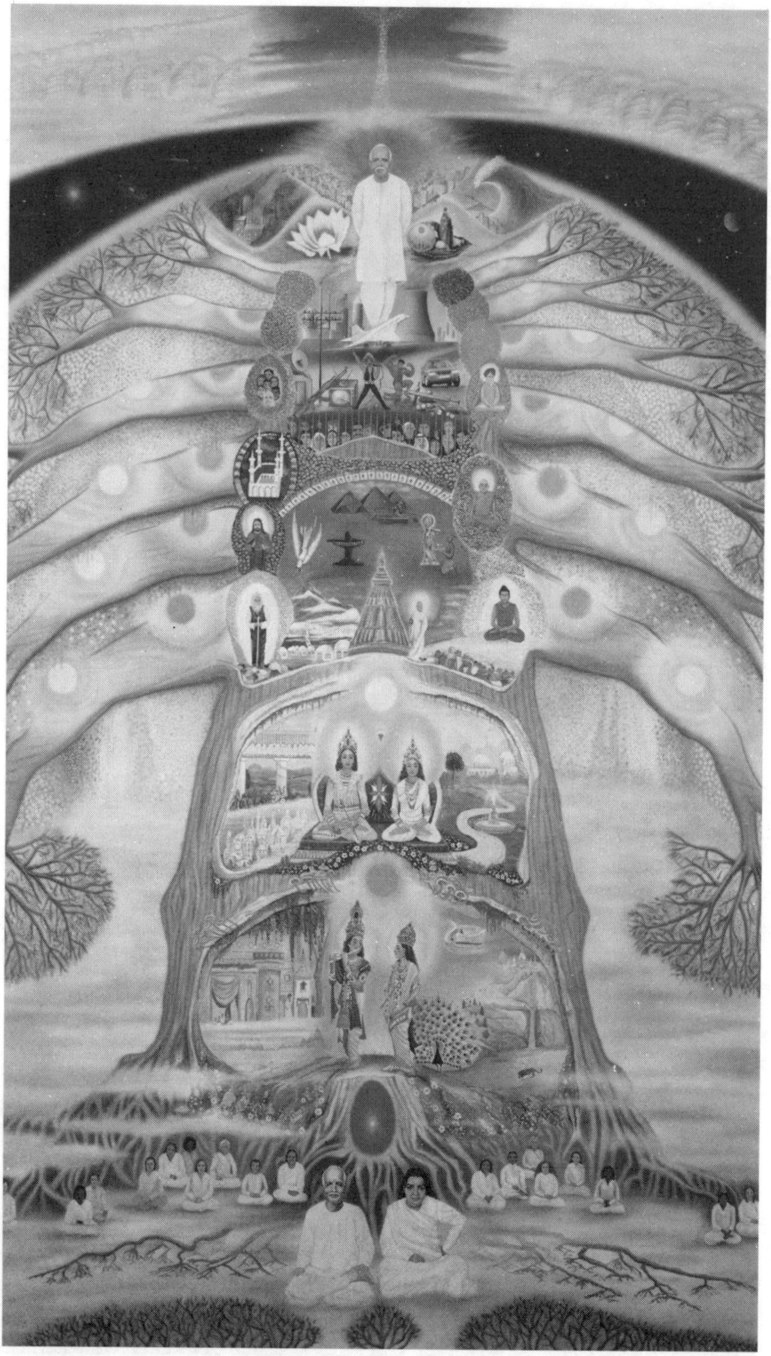

4.2: The Tree of Humanity.

they were 'souls', could go to the soul-world through meditation and be with Shiva Baba as God. Recognising themselves as radiant points of light, as souls, they could through yoga have direct access to the soul-world, and experience abiding there for a while with Shiva Baba in a world of bliss and peace and power.

However in their trances and meditation, and in their reflection on the meaning of the two separate and 'opposed' worlds of matter and soul, the Brahma Kumaris felt the need for another world — a kind of intermediate subtle world that could be seen as a staging post between the body-consciousness of the physical world and the soul-consciousness of the soul-world. Some important trance visions of Dadi Gulzar brought out in greater detail the nature of this intermediate angelic world, and other people were able to have access to it in their own experiences. Furthermore, it was decided that a picture should be made of the three worlds that were now the birthright of the Brahma Kumaris (see illus. 4.1).

The Tree of Humanity

A second important picture was that of a cosmic tree. Brahma Baba described it in a murli at 6.30am in the King Bhavan bungalow. He said that he had been to the subtle (angelic) world and seen a beautiful vision of a cosmic tree. It was so special that he asked a leading brother named Vishwa Ratan to make a design of it. Vishwa Ratan was freed from other duties and given a room to work in. He prepared pencil-drawings for Brahma Baba to approve, and he made ongoing corrections in the light of what Brahma Baba said. He had to think how to make the tree. He sketched the seed coming to earth, the ages emerging, and branches beginning to grow. He put Western developments on one side of the tree, and eastern developments on the other side. It was decided that Brahma Baba should be in the picture, then Om Radhe as well as some of the other Brahma Kumaris. The four-armed Vishnu had to be in the image, too, as should the founders of other religious traditions, and the world war that had recently finished. And so it went on. Finally, Vishwa Ratan was asked to make twelve copies of the cosmic tree in eight days. It seemed impossible but all the pictures were ready in ten days. This picture (see illus. 4.2) was set up as a print in 1950.

The World Cycle

The picture of the world cycle was finished in 1948. It incorporated the four stages of the world, the rise of the main world religions and the four ages: the Brahmanic, Abrahamic, Buddhist and Christian. These four dynasties had supposedly been founded by Brahma Baba himself, Abraham, the

4.3: Shiva Baba (God) as a point of light.

Buddha and Christ. The picture is not strictly accurate. However it was an attempt to take more seriously the other religious traditions of the world.

Shiva Baba

Another important picture, which had earlier depicted Shiva Baba as an egg-shaped cone of light, was changed to present the Supreme Soul as a point of light (see illus. 4.3).

5

Mount Abu

In 1947 British India was partitioned into two independent nations: India in the south, and Pakistan in the north. The latter was now a Muslim country, so the Brahma Kumaris in Karachi had found themselves surrounded by Muslims. Nevertheless, they had been left virtually free to live their own lives.

During their years in Karachi they had undergone intensive training in meditation and knowledge, had become steadfast in self-discipline, had deepened their spiritual awareness and had also achieved a profound understanding of Shiva Baba as the Supreme Soul. In addition, they had started to shape their plans for the future. Outstanding women leaders had emerged, and the willingness of men to work with and under women had been established. Thus the Karachi episode had been important, but now the situation was becoming psychologically different, and it was time to move on.

The Move from Pakistan to India

After soundings had been made over months in 1950, the Brahma Kumaris moved to a rented building on Mount Abu in the Indian state of Rajasthan. This hill station pleasantly situated above the hot plains had for centuries been a pilgrimage centre as it held spiritual vibrations that the Brahma Kumaris claimed to be able to detect. On the mountain was the famous Jain Dilwara temple, with its outstandingly beautiful carved marble, as well as a number of tribal villages.

Moving the Brahma Kumaris and their belongings from Karachi to Mount Abu was stressful as was establishing the community in its new surroundings. During the transition from a life of regular calm and systematic simplicity to a new and still unpredictable life in a different setting, some people fell by the wayside either literally or metaphorically. A core group remained at Mount Abu and began to build for the future. In the first year, while adjustments were being made, the members fell back on an established pattern of life involving meditation, knowledge and communal living to pull them through this difficult period.

Meanwhile relatives and friends who had relocated to India or were already living in India invited the Brahma Kumaris to come and talk about their ideas. The members went in small groups to different places and began their 'spiritual service'. Before long, branches opened in important Indian cities such as Amritsar, Bangalore, Mumbai, Kolkata, Delhi and Lucknow. These centres in turn became vehicles for increasing expansion. What the Brahma Kumaris later came to describe as their commitment to world service had begun.

In addition to speaking about their ideas, and introducing visitors to meditation, the Brahma Kumaris experimented with spiritually helpful ways of using music, which will be mentioned later.

Their dramatic paintings also opened up ways of explaining Brahma Kumari ideas, and new paintings were created to focus on the golden age to come, and on key Hindu figures in the golden age such as Krishna and Radha, and Narayan and Lakshmi. Yet other paintings depicted: Brahma Baba's vision of Vishnu; the subtle angelic region; Om Radhe as Mama; and the mass destruction to come. Later on, these paintings were used at fairs and special events to attract visitors to Brahma Kumari centres. As such sagas, galas, festivals, fairs and presentations are legion in India they became arenas of free advertisement for Brahma Kumari meetings and programmes. It was thus becoming clear that a pictorial sense of evangelism was emerging, and that the incognito phase was now a thing of the past.

The Mount Abu centre continued to grow as a headquarters under the leadership of Brahma Baba, while Om Radhe increasingly took a leading part in its administration. It became clear that the Brahma Kumaris had a gift for administration, and that a concern for spirituality and the growing leadership of women did not diminish but rather heightened their capacity to run things efficiently. This dual emphasis on deep contact with God, and organising matters well in the world has always been a feature of the movement. Moreover, as arrangements stabilised, Om Radhe was freer to tour round India and set up further centres.

Money

In contrast to many new religious traditions, which place great stress on wealth, the Brahma Kumaris avoided any emphasis on money in their spiritual service. Instead they compiled a course of instruction for people interested in their teaching; it would eventually include seven lessons. That course, and those lessons, were free of charge. When people joined the Brahma Kumaris, the money they saved because of their increased simplicity of living was given voluntarily to the movement. Dowries were sometimes received from fathers who understood that their daughters, on joining the Brahma Kumaris, would never marry. In addition, gifts — sometimes anonymous — were received from well-wishers. The money so obtained was used to extend the headquarters at Mount Abu, as most of Lekhraj's original fortune had been dispersed by now. It was also spent elsewhere to obtain properties that became the focal point for local services and activities around India.

At times when major buildings have been bought or built, there has been a generous financial response around the Brahma Kumari world. This is where the family and sharing side of the movement comes into play. For other projects such as the modern hospital built on Mount Abu begun in 1990 a rich industrial company provided a major contribution for the work to start. The hospital is named J. Watumull Memorial Global Hospital and Research Centre with the subtitle 'a temple of health and happiness' (see illus. 5.1). Other charities, industrialists and sponsors gave significant help, and the hospital is thriving. Thus although the Brahma Kumaris World Spiritual University did not provide all the money for the scheme, it gave the great gift and vision of a holistic hospital, aided by serving and practical help from some medically trained Brahma Kumaris.

5.1: J. Watumull Memorial Global Hospital and Research Centre, Mount Abu.

In other ways too, financial help has come. For some large projects food has been provided free of charge and in bulk. In the United Kingdom tax relief is available to the university as it is a charity. Other bodies have sponsored the movement in some of its other activities: for example, significant help since 2004 has been given to annual 'mega events' in India, attracting more than 100,000 people. From May to October 2011 a series of major events was held in Delhi to celebrate the seventy-fifth anniversary of the founding of the Brahma Kumaris movement. Organisations large and small are now more willing to donate to a university that, in their eyes, has proved its worth.

Local Centres

Women were appointed to head the local centres, and if no woman was suitable for such leadership a man could assume this role. The feminine, nurturing type of leadership that evolved at the local centres was based on that shown on Mount Abu itself, where the members of the trust and leading women exemplified a deep, humble and caring notion of spirituality. The extraordinary and moving thing is that very few of these young women had been trained to do a job, to speak in public, to administer anything, to teach, or even to write well. Nor had they travelled much. Yet here they were, like Dadi Gulzar in Lucknow, travelling on her own for the first time to set up a centre in a strange place where she would have to lead men as well as women. Since the age of eight Dadi Gulzar had lived in the shelter of Om Mandli in Hyderabad and then in Karachi, but now she was expected to lead and to speak in public in Lucknow.

The role of these centres was to extend at local level the knowledge and spirituality that was present in a deeper form at Mount Abu. Continued training and guidance were given to the local leaders, who were sent to Mount Abu to share in 'refresher courses' led by Brahma Baba and the women leaders of the movement. The themes remained the same but were given greater focus. They were: the centrality of soul-consciousness rather than body-consciousness; the bodily (but not mental or spiritual) separation of the sexes; the nurturing of the body as a vehicle for the soul; the deepening of a sense of the Supreme Soul through a rigorous yet joyful spirituality; the care for one another and potentially for a wider society as 'souls' who were awakening to their true nature; the secondary nature of money as a tool rather than a master; and the experiential building up of knowledge about the reality of things. The sacred syllable 'Om' was not stressed as much as previously. More deep attention was now being given, at a more mature level, to ongoing basic questions such as 'Who am I?', 'Who is Brahma Baba?' and 'Who is God?' Earlier, 'Om' had been given as a new name to Om Radhe and to other early followers, and it remains in use to this day in the phrase *om **shanti***, a universal greeting given by Brahma Kumaris to one another around the world.

Key Personnel

So far little mention has been made of men in the early work of the Brahma Kumaris, at Mount Abu and elsewhere in India.

An important figure among a number of men who were at ease in the community was Vishwa Kishore, who joined the movement as a brother in the early days. He discovered a promising house and surrounding gardens at Mount Abu and reported this to Brahma Baba, which led to its purchase in 1950. Vishwa helped the Brahma Kumaris to settle in their new home at Madhuban and he took a prominent part in the future evolution of the community.

Jagdish Chander, who was the Brahma Kumaris' official spokesperson and writer, had become a **surrendered member** (that is, committed for life to the Brahma Kumaris) in 1953. He had held a leading position at a teacher training college near Delhi, and since his youth had been interested in religion in general as well as in what would now be called comparative religion. Judaism was little known in India but the Hindu and Muslim traditions, and to a lesser extent the Buddhist one, were known. However Jagdish eventually became involved in Brahma Kumari meditation and spirituality. Through the Brahma Kumaris he found a deep experience of God and he decided to dedicate himself full time to their cause. In graphic accounts he describes how there were occasional sticky times, during the early days, of setting up new centres and taking the message to wider, and usually Hindu, audiences. It was not usual for women to lead in religious matters or indeed in anything. What they were saying was new and unusual. Moreover they were celibate women. They seemed to be somewhat strange and even subversive. Violence was not unusual, and Jagdish himself got beaten up on at least one occasion.

Ramesh Shah also joined the Brahma Kumaris in 1953, when he was a nineteen-year-old student in Mumbai. His father had died in 1950, and his mother had subsided into a three-year melancholy of despair. When a Brahma Kumari centre opened in Mumbai in 1953, his mother decided to visit it and within weeks she was a changed woman. Ramesh was interested in the group that had helped to cure his mother, but was not deeply attached to it at that time. However in 1960 he met Usha while they were both attending Patanjali yoga classes. They decided to marry, and at Usha's suggestion they agreed to share a celibate marriage. In 1961 they went to Madhuban on Mount Abu, and became committed for life to the Brahma Kumaris and to celibacy. Ramesh ran an accounting firm, and he and Usha became firm workers for and supporters of the movement that had so changed his mother, who was never depressed again and lived into her nineties.

Nirwair Singh, a Sikh by birth, was working in the Indian navy and in electronics when he came across the Brahma Kumaris in 1958 in Mumbai and later in Delhi. In Mumbai he met Om Radhe on one of her visits and enjoyed a deep spiritual experience through her. In 1963 he decided to leave the navy and commit his life to the work at Mount Abu. Nirwair modernised Madhuban and promoted building projects within its grounds. He envisaged the design of the impressive Universal Peace Hall (Om Shanti Bhavan, as it was known in Hindi) (see illus. 5.2), and later was an important figure in promoting the design of the Global Hospital on Mount Abu, which would not only help the community at Madhuban but would also provide an up-to-date resource for the whole community on Mount Abu including its tribal villages.

Along with men of ability, a number of capable women also entered the Mount Abu community to bolster the core members who had been involved since Hyderabad and Karachi. They strengthened old centres and founded new ones.

Further Growth

Until 1954 Brahma Kumari operations remained solely in India — contacts with new places being mainly set up by invitations to particular places rather than by random visits to strange cities. The daily murlis, distributed from Mount Abu to the new centres where they were read out by local sisters, formulated and strengthened these ideas within a background of meditation.

Thereafter, more sophisticated methods of outreach were introduced. The Brahma Kumaris felt that these new methods were revealed by God to Brahma Baba. Indeed the whole history of the Brahma Kumari World Spiritual University is held by the Brahma Kumaris to be in response to the initiative of God. However as in the case of the revelations made to Muhammad at Mecca, the visions were relevant to advancing the tradition concerned. In addition to the pictures of the visions given to Brahma Baba, which were commonly featured at the university's centres around India, more elaborate exhibitions began to be organised, and they too were taken round India. Seminars were held and conferences run in different places. A dialogue was initiated with a variety of people and sectors of society, and ideas resulting

5.2: Universal Peace Hall (Om Shanti Bhavan), Mount Abu.

from these interactions fed back into Brahma Kumari consciousness. The time of isolation was slowly receding.

What was not yet passing was the Indian nature of the Brahma Kumari project. The course of lessons and the murlis were in Hindi; and the allusions referred to in the murlis, in the teaching and in the spirituality were Hindu in tone, albeit the ethos of the allusions was transposed into a Brahma Kumari mode. The staff at the Brahma Kumari World Spiritual University were Indian. Anyone committing themself to the university was given a dual piece of advice that sometimes proved incompatible. On the one hand, they were recommended to remain in their family, to be gentle and loving to family members and to treat them as 'souls' on a compassionate basis. On the other hand, new entrants were to be firm in their opposition to body-consciousness in the form of sex. This was, so to speak, the sticking point. Tolerance was possible in other matters but not in regard to body-consciousness.

In a number of cases spouses joined the Brahma Kumaris, as we have seen in the case of Ramesh and Usha Shah, and engaged in a celibate marriage. If there were children already they were accepted within the Brahma Kumari fold. However in cases where the partner was not happy to accommodate the stricture on sex as body-consciousness, the marriage might break up. Clearly this was not helpful to the Brahma Kumaris in the eyes of wider society. It was the classic struggle between spiritual values (whereby a person might be willing to leave a family for the sake of spiritual truth) and social values. Thus, while the Brahma Kumaris sought to keep loving contact with family members as a matter of spiritual love and compassion, there was a potential dilemma in regard to the central notion of body-consciousness.

Two Traumatic Events

The death of Om Radhe in 1965 was especially distressing for the Brahma Kumaris. She was still reasonably young, at the age of forty-five, and her leadership had been vital. At a very young age she had led the movement through a series of difficulties, and it seemed as though she would be able to continue to do that for many more years. It was not to be. What would the future hold now that she had gone?

Fortunately, Sister Manmohini was able to take over as a co-administrative head. The work continued but there was concern about Brahma

5.3: Brahma Baba (Dada Lekhraj), first spiritual leader of the Brahma Kumaris.

Baba who was about eighty-nine years old (illus. 5.3). It was a new situation fraught with potential difficulties, and in theory it became more traumatic when Brahma Baba passed away on 18 January 1969. However by this time a pattern had been set up that would remain and develop, and the passing away was seen as part of the eternal drama. Nevertheless, while in the realm of Brahma Kumari theory Om Radhe and Brahma Baba had been outstanding souls whose bodies and external features were incidental to their real being, there was a true sense of loss as well as a sense of exaltation at their decease. In human terms their leadership and example had been crucial.

Their Legacy

By this time a new daily pattern had been put in place for surrendered souls, which is still followed. Brahma Kumaris are woken up by a recorded piece of music at Mount Abu or in a centre, or less often by an alarm clock in the case of individuals at home. After ablutions there is a time of meditation, usually in a room set aside for such activities. For roughly fifteen minutes it focuses on the theme of 'Who am I?' — the answer being that you are a soul with all the implications thereof. For the next fifteen minutes meditation is on God, on being with God, on listening to God and on practising the presence of God. The final fifteen minutes concentrates on the world, and sending out helpful vibrations into the world. At about 4.45am there might be a drink, and a further round of sleep, and then it is time to go to the local centre at about 6.30am to take part in communal meditation, and to listen to and react to the murli. After that there is breakfast, followed by the work of the day. Wherever possible, for example at Madhuban on Mount Abu, at every hour there is a reminder of the time by means of recorded music, and everything stops for one or two minutes for contemplation of God. Interestingly, the early Puritans also practised this hourly remembrance of God. At Madhuban throughout the day there are lessons for residents and/or visitors as well as the necessary work for maintaining the headquarters. (Gradually something like sixty departments arose to organise the life and work of the expanding headquarters, but this exceptionally effective administrative system was linked integrally into the spirituality lying behind Mount Abu.) In the evening at each centre there is an evening meditation, and often one or more classes. Most members of Brahma Kumaris centres, then and now, go out to work during the day. They feel that their life in the world is informed and made fruitful by their spiritual discipline in the morning, in the evening and at weekends.

Thus, although Om Radhe and Brahma Baba had departed this life, the movement lived on. They had been a father and a mother in various ways.

Indeed they had been the only ones to engage in hugging other Brahma Kumaris. This was only one of the ways in which they had exercised a leadership that was caring and also effective.

By 1969 the Brahma Kumaris had been present in India since 1936. They were now reasonably tolerated by civic authorities and by the establishment. They had made a reasonable advance in numbers of surrendered members, in numbers of centres and in self-confidence. However protests against the movement had persisted, and would continue in a decreasing way into the 1980s. Thereafter they largely ceased.

Yet paradoxically from 1969 onwards, although Om Radhe and Brahma Baba were not there to see it, the movement was destined to grow more rapidly, and Brahma Baba was the major influence in making that possible. The example of his life had been there for all to see. He had been present daily at Madhuban on Mount Abu, available for counsel, encouragement and spiritual empowerment. His visions, teaching and money had been formative in the building up the university. It was through him that the murlis had been received and relayed. To that extent, as in the case of Muhammad, Brahma Baba was the channel of the body of knowledge that constitutes the equivalent of the sacred texts of the university. And yet he had not been and had not seen himself as a guru. He was a mere soul who had been singled out by God to be the medium for the inauguration of a new spiritual movement and of a new message for the world. Paradoxically, Brahma Baba's view about himself would be superseded by religious practice, and after his death a memorial was set up to him at Mount Abu. Thus gradually what amounts to a form of devotion began to be offered to him by some of those among whom he had lived.

6

Expansion

The death of a leader, or in the case of the Brahma Kumaris the death of two leaders, usually represents a time of crisis in the formation of a new religious movement. In the case of Om Radhe and Brahma Baba this did not occur. They were succeeded by a new leader — Dadi Prakashmani — and other co-leaders, and the work not only continued without decline but also began to grow rapidly.

Spread of the Movement Abroad

The first significant overseas centre was set up in London at the beginning of the 1970s, and a gifted leader, Dadi Janki, arrived to guide it (see illus. 6.1). From London there would be expansion into the major cities of the United Kingdom, into continental Europe and into other parts of the world. This growth was gradual but it was also steady. In twenty years, spearheaded partly by and from the London centre, some 212 centres and eighty sub-centres were opened in seventy countries. Anyone joining the community becomes part of a branch of the Brahma Kumaris World Spiritual University, so the university began to grow outside India.

Eventually, in order to organise the extra workload, different zones were created from the 1970s onwards to help out and take over from the London centre. Russia established four centres and three sub-centres, which cared for 800 people. Centres were set up in various African countries — Botswana, Kenya, Madagascar, Malawi, Tanzania, Zambia and Zimbabwe — but their local zone centre was in Kenya, and the whole African set-up became known as the Kenya zone. The London zone served centres in nineteen European countries, together with some outside Europe, including Israel and Dubai. Under the New York zone were centres in Argentina, Barbados, Brazil, Canada, Chile, Colombia, Costa Rica, Guatemala, Guyana, Jamaica, Mexico, Surinam, Trinidad and the United States. The final zone was centred in Australia, with the local zone centre in Sydney; it served

6.1: London Brahma Kumaris in the early days.

a miscellany of centres that ranged as far and wide as Australia itself, Fiji, Hong Kong, Indonesia, Japan, Korea, Malaysia, New Zealand, the Philippines, Singapore, South Africa, Sri Lanka and Thailand.

The London, Delhi, New York and Sydney centres were crucially important in the overall work and expansion of the Brahma Kumaris World Spiritual University. In view of the strict standards of the Brahma Kumaris their growth has been striking. On 9 May 1992, the numbers outside India amounted to 5,715 committed members, and it was clear that the preponderance of Brahma Kumaris was still in India. Nevertheless, the significance of the spread of the Brahma Kumaris into the rest of the world should not be underestimated. Although the numbers were still small, they were swollen considerably by students who were taking the Brahma Kumari course, and by others who were sympathetic but who never fully joined them.

The influx into the Brahma Kumaris World Spiritual University of foreign members had a considerable impact on the movement itself, and its outlook, vocabulary and world-view became less Indian. Members came into significant contact with other religious traditions, especially Christianity and Hinduism, and also encountered Western and other systems of thought such as ecology, holistic health, human potential movements, and Western and other spiritual currents. The agenda, horizon and outlook of the university have therefore been subtly changed by the global scene. Meanwhile the leadership of the Brahma Kumaris remains Indian — and well respected around the world.

Widening Scopes and Horizons

The second area of growth that occurred after the demise of the two leaders was connected with a different kind of expansion within the university, which from 1972 started to run a series of international conferences, spiritual fairs, special-interest seminars and world tours. These included the first of a number of ongoing peace missions in 1973 and world spiritual fairs organised in Bangalore, Mumbai, Kolkata, Delhi and Mysore between 1973 and 1975. Between 1976 and 1980 world conferences were held in India on topics as diverse as 'Divinising man', 'The future of mankind' and 'Human survival'. Furthermore, special-interest seminars were run at Mount Abu on the *Bhagavad Gītā*, the *Mahābhārata*, art, law and yoga. These events were more far-reaching in aim and scope than earlier ones, which had concentrated on India.

A New Source for the Murlis

A third and forced change was made necessary by the death of Brahma Baba in 1969, as the murlis could no longer be delivered by him in person. Thus the university's source of revelation and divine guidance had disappeared. This loss was made good by the blossoming of Dadi Gulzar, who became a trance medium through whom murlis could be delivered and through whom individuals could hear God speaking to them. As the head of the Delhi zone she could also speak in her own right. However on predetermined occasions, she underwent what seemed to be a change of countenance and voice. God came down and spoke through her, according to the Brahma Kumari experience. Although no longer a young woman, for anything up to eight or nine hours she would pass over into a new mode of personality, and appear to become a channel of God to inspire individuals and through whom God could reveal further murlis to the community.

As a result a dual system of murlis came into operation at the morning sessions. Murlis that had been given by Brahma Baba when alive were organised into a rota, and they would continue to be repeated as sacred utterances. They were called ***sakar*** **murlis**. The murlis revealed through Dadi Gulzar were ***avyakt*** **murlis** (literally, subtle murlis) and they were relevant to later situations. These were read out at the morning murli sessions once a week, and later more often.

Bap-Dada

A fourth change that followed the death of Brahma Baba related to his status. He had claimed that he was a soul chosen by God to be a mediating focus in the transition age in which the world was now set. He had always downplayed the idea of devotion (*bhakti*) as a partial concept. However after his death there arose a groundswell of hero-worship towards Brahma Baba. There was a sense that while he was living in a physical body his own view of his own status must be respected, and it would have been wrong to reverence him in a way that was contrary to what he had claimed about himself. After his death, that caveat was no longer relevant. He could be given the honour that had not been appropriate during his life.

It was believed that Brahma Baba had gone to a mid-way realm between the world inhabited by human souls and that occupied by the Supreme Soul, namely God (Shiva Baba). From his subtle, mid-way angelic world, in unison with Shiva Baba he was now visiting places all over earth bestowing godly knowledge, purity and peace to many human souls and undertaking the divine task of re-establishing the golden age. In other words, God and Brahma Baba were operating in a kind of dual way as Bap-Dada, with whom one could connect and by whom one could be jointly blessed. Brahma Baba had become part of a dual focus of devoted remembrance. Likewise, the *avyakt* murlis delivered to Dadi Gulzar could be seen to have been revealed by God along with the now angelic Brahma Baba.

How has this development been viewed by non-Indian believers who have come into the university since Brahma Baba's transition? Some feel that they still want to go straight to God without necessary reference to Brahma Baba, while others see him as a mediating focus to reach God. A third group are happy to accept that God and Brahma Baba are a dual focus of devoted remembrance in the form of Bap-Dada. It may even be an advantage that Brahma Baba has been semi-deified because this makes him important to newcomers in a way that would not have been true had his status remained that of a great soul.

A Closer Look at Some Non-Indian Centres

By 1982 there were 850 Brahma Kumari centres in India and seventy in countries abroad, and the development of those outside India is fascinating.

Activities in London

Work began in London in 1971 and it was guided by two key people — Dadi Janki and Sister Jayanti.

Dadi Janki was born in Sind in 1916 into a wealthy Bhaiband family, who were connected with the family of Brahma Baba. She went to the early *satsangs* at Dada Lekhraj's home and was deeply affected by them. As she received only three years' education she was not in a position to pursue a career or have enough money to look after herself. The norm for people like her was to have an arranged marriage, to bear children and to look after the family. Dadi Janki knew that this was not the life for her, but she was coerced into an arranged marriage in 1937. She was not allowed to have contact with Om Mandli and was forced into sexual relations with her husband, which resulted in a child who died after four months. She eventually escaped to Karachi, and her husband remarried. Dadi Janki then went on to Mount Abu. In the 1950s and 1960s she travelled more extensively in India, managing centres and running classes. However in a vision, and in her general sense of the future, she foresaw that the Brahma Kumaris were destined to go out into the even wider world. From 1969 she had the opportunity to spearhead such an activity, so she is mainly responsible for the advance of the Brahma Kumaris in London and around the world. Dadi Janki commands deep respect around the world, and has received many gifts and honours from various quarters.

Fortuitously her path crossed with that of Sister Jayanti, another woman who was more than thirty years younger than her. Jayanti had been born in Pune (Poona) in 1949 and her mother became a surrendered Brahma Kumari in 1957 just before Jayanti and her parents moved to London. They had already met Brahma Baba and Dadi Janki, and Brahma Baba had recognised Jayanti's leadership qualities. Once in London the family began to hold Brahma Kumari meetings in their house, and Jayanti attended a local grammar school and then London University where she studied pharmacy. She was the only Indian girl in her class at school, and thus she became attuned to the Western way of life. In 1968 Jayanti went back to Pune, where she again met Dadi Janki, who was leading the centre there. While there Jayanti studied Brahma Kumari teachings and realised the deep insights of Dadi Janki. Brahma Baba sent Sister Jayanti — now a dedicated Brahma Kumari — to work in Agra, the home of the Taj Mahal, after which she travelled to Mount Abu and saw Brahma Baba before he died.

Sister Jayanti sensed that she was destined to return to England, and once there she began to prepare the way for Dadi Janki to join her in London. Sister Jayanti had a pleasing temperament and a clear pleasant English accent but was also fluent in Hindi. Her role and promise were becoming clear. Finally in 1974 Dadi Janki was asked to go to London for three months to join Sister Jayanti, and a superb partnership began that would last for much longer than three months. They settled into a small flat, shared initially with another tenant, in Tennyson Road in north-west London. Sister Jayanti was street-savvy, which enabled her to help Dadi Janki, who spoke no English and so needed a translator. In London they put on an exhibition of Brahma Kumaris pictures.

Some westerners began to attend the morning class and evening meditation in the flat, which doubled as a centre. Two of the first group to take the seven-day course became surrendered Brahma Kumaris, and one of them travelled to Madhuban on Mount Abu as part of the first group from abroad to visit this distant place.

Although it was becoming clear that Dadi Janki should remain in London, it was not ideal for an elderly Indian lady to live in a cold climate, knowing no English and sharing a flat. Fortunately, an adjacent house became available and was purchased, although Dadi Janki remained in the flat. Meanwhile a good number of people were coming to the morning class and partaking in the seven-day course.

By the end of 1974 Sister Sudesh had arrived from India as a long-term team leader who would serve in London for a number of years, before transferring to Germany, and then travelling around the rest of the world.

Expansion in the United States

Meanwhile in the United States another team of able and dedicated women — Mohini Panjabi and Gayatri Naraine — were emerging on the scene. They were more modern in outlook, well educated and attuned to Western working practices. Their parents came from a diplomatic background, and Mohini was a diplomatic journalist and Gayatri a university administrator.

Mohini was born in 1940, and she first came across the Brahma Kumaris when aged eleven. Her family were living in Delhi and in 1957 she met Brahma Baba when he visited that city. She decided in principle to become a Brahma Kumari but first she studied history and political science at university and gained a journalism diploma. From 1963 Mohini began living in Brahma Kumari centres while doing her work, and in the Delhi centre she had contacts with foreign embassies. Because she was an English speaker, in 1974 she went to London and helped Dadi Janki. Then she moved to Canada and the USA, where there had been no Brahma Kumari centres. From there she was asked by Dadi Prakashmani to go to the Caribbean, where she began to set up centres. Finally, in 1977, she settled in New York City, where, in the Queens area, she established one of the first US centres.

She was soon joined there by Gayatri Naraine, who had been born in Guyana into an Indian family. At the time Guyana was under British rule. Although Gayatri was Indian, she belonged to the English-speaking elite and had sympathy for the indigenous black Afro-Caribbeans. Her father, Steve Naraine, later became a minister in the Guyana Parliament, and eventually vice-president of the country. The first Brahma Kumari centre in Guyana opened in 1976. It was accessible to Indians, British and Afro-Caribbeans alike, and it was here that Gayatri came to believe that spirituality, peaceful co-existence, a global outlook and opportunities for women were of universal importance. A year later she went to join Mohini Panjabi in the New York centre, which was a short ride away from the United Nations headquarters.

Mohini already had diplomatic contacts at the United Nations, and Liz Hodgkinson tells the amusing story of how Mohini and Gayatri turned up at the UN reception desk, wearing their white Brahma Kumari robes and desiring to see a certain official (Hodgkinson, 2002, p. 118). A message was passed on to the official concerned to the effect that 'two angels' were waiting to see him, and he had better come down as soon as possible! The eventual result of their excellent work, done through long official channels, was that in 1980 the Brahma Kumaris became affiliated to the UN Department of Public Information as a Non-Governmental Organisation (NGO). After the first step of affiliation to the UN there was the desire to go deeper and to become still more involved at the UN. The outcome was that in 1983 a deeper consultative status was afforded to them on the roster of the Economic and Social Council of the UN. This was upgraded to General Consultative Status in 1998. The Brahma Kumaris were the first eastern spiritual body to obtain such recognition.

Non-Indian Conferences

From 1980 to 1982 a special Ten-Point Programme for World Welfare was drawn up by the Brahma Kumaris. This expressed a desire and a perceived call to become more deeply involved in global matters, and this kind of involvement accelerated after 1982. World tours were undertaken by leaders of the movement, and in 1983 the first major non-Indian conference was held on 'The origin of peace' at Nairobi in Africa. In 1983 the first Universal Peace Conference was organised at Mount Abu, and it was followed by others on a yearly basis. In 1984 Dadi Prakashmani was awarded the UN Peace Medal. Smaller international conferences were also held in London on 'The spirit of humanity', in Cologne on 'International science' and in Dublin, Paris, Sydney, New York, Malaysia, Brazil and Colombia on 'Peace'.

The Universal Peace Hall

To attract Western and other foreign visitors to Mount Abu required particular consideration over food, privacy, electrical gadgets and cultural considerations. Nirwair Singh therefore made a fact-finding journey to the West in order to find out how to expand the facilities at Madhuban to make them more suitable. The Universal Peace Hall on Mount Abu, which opened in 1983, was then based on his recommendations as well as those made in the murlis. The hall could accommodate 3,000 people, and it had elaborate simultaneous-translation machines covering more than a dozen foreign languages. Such a facility strengthened the possibility of having international conferences in India which non-Brahma Kumaris and well-known speakers from abroad could attend. It was a new kind of project in India at the time.

The Million Minutes for Peace Project

In India, where opposition had sometimes been strong in local areas and even among higher echelons of society, a change was taking place. In the early 1980s the president G. Z. Singh began to take an interest in and to visit Mount Abu, and this opened up the possibility for other senior government officials to begin to do the same. A little later a Hindu ***Shankaracharya*** made a visit, and this was a breakthrough on the Hindu front. There were also signs that inter-faith contacts were becoming more possible.

In 1983 Sister Manmohini passed away. She had been an able and appreciated leader. Her place as co-administrative head with Dadi Prakashmani was taken by Dadi Janki.

As the International Year of Peace approached in 1986, the Brahma Kumaris began to consider what contribution they could make to that important year. Would it be possible to think of something out-of-the-ordinary that would be of deep interest around the world? Inspiration came from Australia where in 1985 three members hit on the notion of encouraging people elsewhere to spend minutes thinking about peace and ideas that would contribute to peace. This would not require money nor material gifts, but it would involve time and mental effort. If enough people joined a project of this kind the outcome would be not only odd minutes for peace but also a Million Minutes for Peace collected and shared by citizens from many nations. These young Australians contacted Madhuban and the idea was accepted.

In this simple and unexpected way what became known as the Million Minutes for Peace project began, and the arrangements spread around the world. However as far as Madhuban was concerned there were four potential problems. In the first place they was no one who had experience of enormous ventures such as the Million Minutes for Peace project, and in any case there were relatively few people at Madhuban. Secondly, money was in short supply. The financial situation was better than it had been but it was not totally secure, and there were few if any financial experts living at Madhuban to source the money needed. They therefore needed help from wealthy donors and from experts in organisation in order realistically to tackle a project such as the Million Minutes for Peace. Where would they come from? Thirdly, how would it be possible to contact wealthy donors and set up communication networks to finance and publish such an extraordinary scheme? And finally, their two leaders – Dadi Prakashmani and Dadi Janki – were seventy and sixty-five years of age. Could they cope?

These problems were overcome in different ways. The two leaders gave wholehearted support. In London a team of young, dedicated and energetic professionals, including an advertising agent (Mike George) and a journalist (Nichola Malet de Carteret), set about planning a campaign centred on marketing, recruiting volunteers and spreading enthusiasm for the project. It was ingenious and successful. Mohini Panjabi and Gayatri Naraine aroused interest and approval at the United Nations in New York in what was seen as an unusual and important scheme. A co-ordinating office in St John's Wood, London was loaned freely, and its attractive environment was of real help. Other co-ordinating centres were set up in New York, Sydney (Australia) and Nairobi (Kenya). The aim was to seek services, materials, facilities, posters, advertising channels and so on that could be offered cheaply and easily, so money was not required. In addition, packs were assembled and dispatched to organisations and schools in order to rouse interest and possible help (see illus. 6.2). Moreover they were offered help by influential people who were not members of the Brahma Kumaris but who appreciated the work that they were doing: for example, Lord Ennals, a former British Labour minister and advocate for peace, offered a room in the British House of Lords for the first meeting of the British Million Minutes for Peace committee. Dozens of other well-known patrons emerged ranging from Ben Kingsley, Deborah Kerr and Paul McCartney to Yehudi Menuhin, Mother Teresa and Margaret Thatcher. Countless other people around the world, including the present writer, did not give direct help but were able to indicate their moral support.

Although the project was supported by religious people, its aim was to secure a much wider audience. The possible contributions to the actual programme included minutes of dedicated thinking about peace, silent meditations on peace, and prayers for peace. There were different possibilities ranging from repeating contributions day after day for a committed length of time to offering a short or a long session on one particular day. It was also possible to support the cause by means of music, art, vision statements and so on. In the end, it was decided that a month should be set aside for the appeal itself, namely 16 September to 16 October 1986. In all eighty nations took part, and 1,231,975,713 minutes were collected from eighty-eight countries. The final celebration took place in the Cathedral of St John

6.2: Terry Waite with schoolchildren and the Million Minutes of Peace bus.

the Divine in New York on 22 October 1986. At the end of it the congregation carried lighted candles into the darkness of New York.

The paradox about the Million Minutes of Peace project is that the body who organised it did not seek gratification or recognition from it, and their name was printed in only tiny type in much of the literature so that a number of people were not aware of the crucial part played by the Brahma Kumaris. It was they who had envisaged and co-ordinated the appeal, yet they did not receive the acclaim they deserved. However the United Nations did award the Brahma Kumaris the title of Peace Messenger, and in 1987 they gained seven more Peace Messenger Awards from the United Nations. These did make them better known, as marginally did their Golden Jubilee celebrations in 1987.

In 1988 the Brahma Kumaris became involved in another scheme entitled Global Co-operation for a Better World. It was launched in April in the Houses of Parliament in London. This was a kind of follow-up event to the Million Minutes one. Again, this did not involve seeking money but it did require a similar battery of helpers, projects and global participation. It sought widespread notions of what a better world might mean, what it might be like and how it might be able to move forward on a global basis. Ideas on paper, in pictures and photographs, in films and in other media were collected and stored from around the world. Ideals, hopes and aspirations for a better world were received from people in 122 nations. They were eventually put into a database that was given the name of the Global Co-operation Bank. This put into the public arena a more positive and creative view of the future as opposed to the often more dismal views that were peddled elsewhere.

The basic ideas set out in the Global Co-operation Bank were also summarised in the Mount Abu Declaration, which became part of the Brahma Kumari vision. This stated that what was needed was: a spirit of co-operation and goodwill; an attitude of love and respect towards each other; the practice of positive and creative thinking; the application of moral and spiritual values in daily life; and action based on a shared vision of a better world (see illus. 6.3). And yet the Brahma Kumari dilemma remained — and remains — a conundrum. If Brahma Baba's visions of an apocalyptic end to the world that would prepare the way for a new golden age still remained valid, how could it be united with Global Co-operation for a Better World if the old world was so forlorn and due to pass away?

6.3: Tree of Positive Virtues/The good seeds of life.

By then, the Brahma Kumaris had entered the computer age both in the West and in India. Instantaneous communication therefore became increasingly common in centres around the world, and there were more opportunities for every member to feel part of a family, and to know what was happening elsewhere. Their work and activities in various parts of the world could now be known everywhere.

Global Hospital Trust

By now the Madhuban headquarters on Mount Abu had enlarged premises to accommodate the growing number of visitors who wished to stay as believers or as honoured guests. In a cupboard at Mount Abu medals were beginning to accumulate presented by dignitaries and others in recognition of the greater service that was being offered to wider communities. Bridges were being built with the Hindu tradition so that the old suspicion, although not completely banished, was being transmuted into respect. Contacts were also being made with people holding political, social and intellectual influence. New developments, including major projects at Mount Abu, helped this welcome change in attitude.

For many years a hospital on Mount Abu was needed for the residents of Madhuban, for the villagers living on the mountain and for visitors to the mountain resort. In 1988 Dadi Gulzar developed cancer. She was well treated by a surgeon in Mumbai and after a successful operation she underwent an ongoing programme of chemotherapy that turned out to be successful. But what if she had been on Mount Abu? Dadi Gulzar's surgeon therefore visited Madhuban and gave advice on healthcare and medical personnel. Nirwair Singh, who had had a heart-bypass himself, also agreed to help in a significant way.

The provision of medical facilities created a new dilemma for Madhuban. Not only were great amounts of money needed to build a decent hospital on the mountain but also paid medical experts would be required to run the facility. In the end it was agreed that spiritual work was and would remain free of charge whereas bodily or physical work could receive monetary backing. In 1989 therefore the Global Hospital Trust was formed. The use of the word 'global' was a continuation of the sense that the Brahma Kumari work and scope had gone in principle beyond India into every reachable corner of the world, including the tribal villagers on Mount Abu, who would now receive relevant medicines and expert healthcare.

The new hospital was a fine example of holistic medicine — its programme included ayurveda Indian medicine, acupuncture, aromatherapy and magnet therapy. There was also daily meditation for staff and patients.

Its high standards incorporated modern and high-tech treatments. A little distance from Madhuban, the hospital was situated in harmony with the surrounding trees, the panoramic views and the beauties of that part of the mountain. Initially it had eight beds but has since grown in size and scope and is a great asset to Mount Abu. It was named the J. Watumull Memorial Global Hospital and Research Centre after the Watumull Brothers whose first large donation triggered the enterprise (see illus. 5.1, p. 51)

Global Co-operation House

Meanwhile in London the original community that had begun in Tennyson Road had mushroomed very significantly and was situated in the Dudden Hill Lane Community Centre. By now hundreds of people, both Indians and Westerners, were attending the morning meetings to listen to the murlis and to take courses, so a number of other centres were established in small houses. Major events that attracted a thousand or more visitors were farmed out to larger premises. It was therefore essential that London should have a centre that was relevant to its growing work, which now stretched not only over London and the rest of the United Kingdom but also into the wider world.

An appropriate building was eventually opened after a series of fortuitous events. A suitable site, with a building on it, was located in Pound Lane, London. It belonged to All Souls College, Oxford, which was asking around £100,000 for its lease. Through Dr Edward Carpenter (a friend of the Brahma Kumaris) All Souls College sold the freehold to the Brahma Kumaris for less than half the original price. In 1988 the original building was demolished, and two sympathetic architects provided plans for a new one, free of charge. The money to pay for Global Co-operation House, which cost four million pounds to build, was found in a variety of ways, especially through the goodwill of Brahma Kumaris around the world. In September 1991 this magnificent new centre was opened. It was ideal for hosting significant events in London as well as for accommodating a welter of local activities.

At the opening of Global Co-operation House Lord Ennals expressed his admiration for the work of the Brahma Kumaris, which was a welcome contrast to the criticisms of the earlier years of the movement, especially in India. He said:

> The opening of Global Co-operation House will be the climax but by no means the end of a great international initiative. Starting with the Million Minutes of Peace during the UN

International Year of Peace, and then the planning of Global Co-operation as a worldwide project, between us we have been able to involve, through their minds and hearts, millions of people across the globe.

This concept of creating not only the vision of a better world, but an action plan to achieve it, owes everything to the Brahma Kumaris. It was their inspiration, their organisation, their enthusiasm, and indeed their vision that have brought us all together as part of a great international project.

Global Co-operation House will be the international centre of the Brahma Kumaris, and for all those who work with them. It will be a source of inspiration for us all. It has my blessings, and that of all the millions of people whose hearts and minds have been led to peace and co-operation (Hodgkinson, 2002, pp. 163–4).

Residential Retreats

Also in the United Kingdom a permanent residential retreat centre was established after a large but somewhat dilapidated building became available outside Oxford at Nuneham Park. It was set in beautiful grounds just outside the village of Nuneham Courteney. Its peaceful surroundings not far from London had the additional advantage of being in the area where Prebendary Marcus Braybrooke, a prominent inter-faith leader, was the local Church of England vicar. He was sympathetic to the Brahma Kumaris and was a helpful local personality. Financially, the Brahma Kumaris were fortunate and, as they would say, led by God.

The UK building had been an eighteenth-century aristocratic mansion with more than forty residential rooms as well as other fine facilities. It had been taken over by the Royal Air Force during the Second World War, had been sold to Oxford University in 1957, had been used as a residential training college from 1968 and had been leased to Rothmans in 1978. They had sold it for £5 million to a hotel company which went bankrupt, so the property was in the hands of receivers. The Brahma Kumaris negotiated a 120-year lease of the property for a bargain price, and spent many thousands of pounds on fully restoring it. The Oxford Global Retreat Centre was opened in 1993 and since then many conferences, retreats, lectures, residential discussions, seminars and so on have been held there. The retreat centre has been a source of enlightenment and help for many people inside and outside of the Brahma Kumaris movement. It is fulfilling its remit as part of a 'spiritual university'. Manda Patel became and remains the leader of the retreat centre, and a feature of it is the new communal practice of men and women living in the same building. This had not happened before in the UK, but was necessary as members of both sexes were needed to organise and run the elaborate work of the centre.

Over in the United States the local centres also needed a residential national retreat centre. It took them some time to source the right place, but by 1999 they had found a site in the Catskill Mountains of Upper New York State. Although it had cost $9 million to buy and furnish in the 1950s, the Brahma Kumaris acquired it for $2.1 million, again a bargain. Within two years, partly by their own efforts, the American Brahma Kumaris transformed the site from being a holiday saloon, gambling bar, nightclub, shooting range and swimming centre to a retreat centre with a large reception area, huge dining-room, good kitchen, massive auditorium and facilities to house 200 guests. As elsewhere, all the routine work of welcoming, cooking, cleaning, decorating and so on was done by the retreat centre's Brahma Kumari residents. The Peace Village, as it became known, is not palatial after the style of the Oxford retreat centre yet it has been adapted in a sensible way into the environment of the beautiful Upper New York milieu, and it serves a similar need to the Oxford centre.

In the Indian (not Pakistani) city of Hyderabad an Academy for a Better World named Shanti Sarovar was established in [2004] as a seat of deep experience and higher learning in values, self-development, meditation, peace of mind and divine wisdom. It offers residential and one-day retreats and fellowship courses in anger and emotion control, harmony in relations, journeys within, leadership attitudes, life-managing skills, living values, positive thinking, raja-yoga meditation, self-esteem, self-managing skills and stress management. In addition to offering tailor-made courses, Shanti Sarovar is also available for use by corporations, institutes or organisations. It has a calm, natural and serene environment that is enhanced by beautiful fountains, gardens, rock formations and waterfalls. All this is organised, as the leaders put it, to create better people for a better tomorrow. As a *A World in Transition Statement* puts it:

> A person who really understands his or her own inherent worth and that of others will come to know that worth is not something given by the world but comes from a source that transcends all that is physical (BKWSU, 1995, p. 8).

New Buildings at Mount Abu

Back at Madhuban a larger auditorium named Diamond Hall, which is part of the Shantivan complex, was built in 1996 further down Mount Abu at Taleti (see illus. 6.4). It could accommodate up to 25,000 people (half sitting and half standing). It was here that crowds of people would arrive on set occasions to hear Dadi Gulzar reveal new murlis from Bap-Dada. Everyone present, men and women, would wear white clothes. Dadi Gulzar would enter and sit down on a seat with an arrangement of cushions. The necessary technical arrangements of microphones and television monitors would be adjusted in the hall and around the walls, and there would be silence. After about half-an-hour Dadi Gulzar would go into a trance. Speaking in an unusual whisper she would transmit the latest murli to the assembled audience. It would ultimately be sent around all the centres of the world as an *avyakt* murli.

On Mount Abu also, on a 23-acre site about three miles from the university's headquarters, another building named Gyan Sarovar (Lake of Knowledge) was opened in 1995 (see illus. 6.5). It contains their Academy for a Better World, which accommodates 1,200 people. It has two large auditoriums, thirteen training units, a library, playgrounds, an environment park, a museum, an art gallery and an alternative energy development building as well as a lab and research section. The academy's brochure states that the Brahma Kumaris World Spiritual University has its focus on understanding the self, its inner resources and strength, and also on developing attributes of leadership and the highest level of personal integrity. The university's

6.4: A gathering of 25,000 Brahma Kumars and Brahma Kumaris in the Diamond Hall auditorium, Mount Abu.

6.5: The Gyan Sarovar complex, Mount Abu.

activities are grounded in the belief that the world needs to invest more resources in educating its peoples with sound human, moral and spiritual values. Thus it is not enough to theorise about values and ethics in institutions, systems and constitutions, for even the best arrangements are of little use if the people who implement them have wrong values.

Near the Shantivan complex, a sister organisation of the Brahma Kumaris named the World Renewal Spiritual Trust, in conjunction with the Frauhofer Institute, in 2010 started to build a solar thermal power plant, which is now the second largest of its kind in the world. The involvement of a formerly fairly secretive body in a project of this type is surely unique.

Inter-Faith Dialogue

An interesting newer channel for Brahma Kumari involvement has been in the field of inter-faith dialogue. In 1985 I was invited to form and lead the Edinburgh Inter-faith Association. The founding religious traditions were the Baha'is, Brahma Kumaris, Buddhists, Christians, Hindus, Jews, Muslims, Sikhs and Unitarians. For a number of years on a Sunday summer afternoon once a year, a procession was organised through the streets of Edinburgh involving people from all religions. It would pause along the way at the buildings of three traditions for refreshments, for conversation, for a talk about each place visited, and for meditation and/or prayer. Sister Louisa Gupta, from the Edinburgh Brahma Kumari Centre, organised that procession for many years on behalf of the association. Especially memorable was the procession in the week of the New York 9/11 outrage in 2001. This was arranged for a Saturday and would involve visits to the Pakistani mosque, a

Church of Scotland church and the Buddhist centre in Portobello. Earlier in the week, a smoke bomb was thrown into the Pakistani mosque, which blackened all its walls that are normally white. Luckily it was not an explosive bomb. The first thought was to abandon the procession. But after discussions it was decided to go ahead and make the event bigger than ever. Therefore on the Saturday more than a hundred people from different religious traditions gathered in the smoke-blackened mosque in solidarity with the local Muslims in their time of need. Brahma Kumari Sister Louisa had organised and approved this.

The Brahma Kumaris have also intensified their participation in inter-faith matters. They have worked with and shared with inter-faith bodies including the International Inter-faith Centre, Respect — It's About Time, the Scottish Inter-faith Council, United Religions Initiative UK, the World Conference of Religions for Peace, the World Congress of Faiths, the Year of Inter-Religious Understanding and Co-operation, and the Young Jains. In view of the early mistrust of other religious traditions, which was partly due to their own 'persecution' by others, their present warmth towards other faith communities represents a remarkable turn-around. Especially fascinating is the increasing rapprochement between the Hindu community and the Brahma Kumaris, where relations are now much more friendly both in India and abroad.

Other Outreach Projects

In more recent years there has also been an intensification of the Brahma Kumaris' work with community organisations. The Prince of Wales summed up their help to his own Prince's Trust in a written commendation:

> Over the last eighteen months, The Brahma Kumaris World Spiritual University has become a strong ally of one of my principal charities, The Prince's Trust, working with them to encourage understanding between the UK's faith communities. In particular, this work, entitled 'Respect', is doing much to help young people find purpose and direction in their lives by making a gift of time to someone in another community. This has the effect of strengthening those bonds of tolerance that are such an important part of civilised society (BKWSU, n.d., p. 2).

In addition to their working with the Prince's Trust, the Brahma Kumaris have helped other groups in similar ways, particularly concerning spirituality and young people. These include the Foundation for Outdoor Adventure, the John Muir Trust, the Rank Foundation and the Stoneleigh Group.

The Janki Foundation for Global Healthcare, founded in December 1997, was named after Dadi Janki. Its aims are to establish a holistic and reflective approach to healthcare for the twenty-first century, and to support the work of the Global Hospital and Research Centre at Mount Abu. Dadi Janki herself, together with Dadi Gulzar and other leading Brahma Kumaris, were greatly helped at times of deep need by orthodox medicine, and her Foundation aims at combining the best elements of medicine in a holistic fashion. It was launched at the Royal College of Physicians in London, and its patron was Lord Norrie, and its first chairman Dr Ray Bhatt. Its first working group meetings took place in the House of Lords in London.

Meanwhile at the Oxford Global Retreat Centre, in addition to internal Brahma Kumaris events, residential seminars have been arranged for numbers of professional groups including architects, care workers, educators, health workers, prison workers, scientists, senior management, social workers and youth workers. Since 2000 more than 500 retreats have been held — seventy-four community events were run in 2002 alone. This represents an extraordinary opening up to and welcoming in of people from other walks of life and other faith traditions. Other retreat centres have also been established in other parts of the world.

Another facet of this openness to others lies in the caring work offered to people in real need in wider society. Initially, the Brahma Kumaris was perceived as members of an élite group interested in the more prosperous elements in society. That had been their own background in the Hyderabad Bhaibund community. Their experiences in Hyderabad and Karachi made them introspective. Since the 1980s the Brahma Kumaris have been going in the opposite direction — giving help to prisoners, drug addicts, youngsters in need through lectures, talks, meditations and personal advice. Advice is offered in a strong yet gentle way about how to overcome unhelpful habits, hurtful behaviour from others, shyness and lack of learning. A former respected member of the British Parliament, Paul Boateng, comments kindly on this aspect of their work:

> The work of the Brahma Kumaris in promoting the values of spirituality, tolerance, peace and reconciliation is to be commended. The Brahma Kumaris have had a key role to play worldwide in providing help, education and support to many of the most disadvantaged and challenged in society and long may that work continue (BKWSU, n.d., p. 16).

Yet another innovation in the early twenty-first century has been the establishment of Inner Space centres in, for example, Cambridge,

Chelmsford, Covent Garden (London) and Glasgow. These centres set in the heart of cities provide havens of peace, quiet and calm away from the hurly-burly of urban life. A brochure comment by a senior lecturer in science, D. Novakovic, outlines the help that these centres give:

> About two years ago I discovered a little gem in the heart of London filled with insights, learning and calm. This was the Inner Space in Covent Garden, a meditation centre that offers courses such as Positive Thinking, Stress Management, Self Esteem and Meditation. It's a friendly shop that sells books, CDs and other products to motivate and make the whole journey of self-development easy. They have a quiet room tucked away with relaxing music and comfortable chairs. This is truly a rare spot in the urban madness that I regularly visit to recover and refresh my energy. The weekly lectures with different speakers on varied topics offer an interesting and inspirational outlook on life, relationships and realisation. Now here comes the best bit — it's all free and the only string attached is you need time and an interest in creating breathing space to unwind! (BKWSU, n.d., p. 12)

A comment in the last quotation stresses an important element in the Brahma Kumaris' work — namely that it is free.

Service Wings, set up in the present century by the Brahma Kumaris, offer courses for various sections of society and they are especially popular in India but operate as well throughout the world. They are seventeen Wings: Administrator's; Art and Culture; Business and Industry; Education; Jurists; Media; Medical; Politicians; Religious; Rural; Scientists and Engineers; Security; Social Service; Sports; Transport; Women's; and Youth.

A project entitled 'Empowering Young People across the World' summarises a vast number of projects for youth that are taking place repeatedly in Australia, Brazil, Canada, Dubai, Germany, Greece, Iceland, India, Japan, Kenya, Mauritius, Russia, Singapore, Spain, Switzerland, Thailand, Trinidad, United Kingdom, USA and Vietnam. The aim of this large group of youth co-ordinators is:

> ... not to seek converts to the Brahma Kumaris but to help people to locate their inner selves and use this connection to inform and support the work they do in the world. As another young person put it 'a good result for me was when someone

left our conference and said that they had arrived with a lukewarm view of their faith and left with a deep knowledge that they were Christian' (Green, 2008, p. 2).

7

Implications of the Changes

The Brahma Kumaris movement now has a global outreach into more than a hundred countries incorporating over 8,500 centres and over 900,000 people. How has this affected their world-view? How have they accommodated their basic ideas, which were formed at an early stage in the movement, to their current prominent global stage? What has happened in the world outside India?

In the wider world, and especially in the West, the Brahma Kumaris have made extensive contact with a variety of people. Their philanthropic and social outreach work into wider society has received many warm tributes including one by the former Mayor of London, Ken Livingstone:

> Having visited Global Co-operation House on a number of occasions, I am well aware of the valuable work that is being undertaken at the BKWSU to develop multi-cultural, multi-faith initiatives to benefit the community to work together in a spirit of peaceful understanding. Therefore I am delighted to have this opportunity to wish the centre every continued success in the future (BKWSU, n.d., p. 4).

David Hemery, an Olympic gold medallist and recent president of UK Athletics, comments:

> People have started to question the purpose of values in society today. Recognising that we are spiritual beings, acting in a physical body, is an important insight. It removes the divisions of race, creed and gender. I hope that the Diamond House addition to Global Co-operation House will provide an added opportunity to raise the consciousness of more people (BKWSU, n.d., p. 6).

The Advance Party

Generally in religious history there are breakaway movements that go back to what they see as the fundamental origins of a tradition, and there are others that adapt to changing situations. Such a divergence of opinion occurred in the Brahma Kumaris when opposition of a fundamentalist type developed in the late 1960s. It was led by the Advance Party, which the Brahma Kumaris call the Shankar Party or Adhyatmik Ishwariya Vishva Vidyalaya. It claims that, by embracing the wider world, the Brahma Kumaris have strayed too far from the original message and this has led to greater worldliness and an unhelpful alliance with worldly leaders and figures of influence. The Advance Party also believes there is too great a discrepancy between what it suggests to be the basic world-view of the Brahma Kumaris, and the movement's closer engagement with other spiritual groups and religious traditions.

From one viewpoint therefore the Advance Party is a reforming group that wishes to reject the striking (and in their view 'corrupt') events and growth of recent times by reverting to the pristine truth and simplicity of the beginnings. On the other hand, it can also be seen as a fundamentalist group that is unable to alter in any way to a passing and negative world.

The Advance Party comprises mainly ex-members of the Brahma Kumaris. Walliss suggests that after Brahma Baba's death in 1969 the movement began to move in a different direction:

> There was a visible change in the attitude of the sisters of various centres and wealthy students were given preference over the not-so-wealthy ones. The power-crazy Brahmins (i.e. the Brahma Kumaris) slowly became commercial as money started pouring in by ignorant students, who are still taken for a ride in the name of God. In fact the whole organisation has now become a true Ravan Rajya where pomp and show and grandeur are given preference over true godly knowledge (Walliss, 2002, p. 113).

He goes on to say that:

> God Shiva will be revealed through the person who becomes the Lord of the weak and poor ... Dada Lekhraj is the Lord of the BKs who are at present the richest and most powerful spiritual organisation in this world (Walliss, 2002, p. 113).

These claims do not sit well with the fact that the Brahma Kumaris (who in Brahma Baba's time were more elitist) have recently moved in the direction of aiding the weak and the poor, as opposed to neglecting them. It is also fair to point out that they themselves live a frugal life, that their meetings are free, and they are very far from being the richest and most powerful spiritual organisation in this world. Indeed it is likely that many people, including some of the people reading this book, may scarcely have heard about the Brahma Kumaris before.

Other Advance Party websites project a somewhat different historical past. The claim is made that, although Dada Lekhraj was an early important figure, he was not the only founder of the Brahma Kumaris. They suggest that Dada Lekhraj's own business partner, named Sevak Ram, was himself the corporeal medium of Shiva Baba. They go on to state that Sevak Ram not only interpreted Lekhraj's visions to him but was also involved with Dada Lekhraj in setting up Om Mandli at its inception, together with another person known as Geeta Mata. Nevertheless, differences arose between him and Dada Lekhraj. Sevak Ram left the movement and died in 1942. The Advance Party agree that Shiva Baba continued to speak to the world through Dada Lekhraj between 1942 and 1969. However they claim that after Dada Lekhraj's death in 1969 Shiva Baba manifested himself through a new medium named Ravendra Dev Dixit. In other words, from that time onwards, God and Dada Lekhraj as Bap-Dada did not communicate to future followers through Dadi Gulzar as their trance medium. Shiva Baba's medium of manifestation was now Ravendra Dev Dixit, who retired to his home village of Kampil in Uttar Pradesh from 1982 to continue his work. It seems fair to comment that there is flimsy evidence for all this.

The Advance Party supplies specific dates for the apocalypse, for the end of the world as it is now known. According to its websites, from 2004 to 2008 Ravendra Dev Dixit was to be 'pronounced' the Father of Humanity and between 2006 and 2008 the whole world would experience a heaven on earth before its destruction. After the destruction in 2008, a population would be built up of 900,000 souls by the beginning of the golden age in 2036. That year would see the centenary of the confluence age begun by the setting up of Om Mandli in 1936, and this new golden age would begin with the coronation of Krishna known as Shri Narayan. By 2011 however none of these events had come to pass.

The Advance Party also accuses the Brahma Kumaris of changing or abandoning some of the murlis when they were written down. This is true, but because the murlis are read out in cycles some are archaic and to leave these in, as they stand, in the twenty-first century might be difficult. Therefore minor adjustments are in order to ensure a meaningful 'scripture'.

Attracting People to the Brahma Kumaris

Unlike the Advance Party, the Brahma Kumaris have adapted to changing world situations, but in what ways? A helpful approach is to analyse which different kinds of people are making contact with them. In India, and among Indians in the West, some knowledge of the Hindu tradition is probable. That is not the case among non-Indians who are not able to fit the Brahma Kumaris into the Hindu context so the situation outside India, especially that in the West, will first be examined. There the Brahma Kumaris are a new and little known phenomenon. As far as sex and age are concerned, in most places more women than men are attracted to the Brahma Kumaris, and the women (and men) comprise all ages. The women and men are generally middle class although more young people, more poorer people and more needy people are becoming involved.

An initial attraction to the movement outside India may be to enhance self-confidence. The interest of people with this motive is to gain help in improving their lives and to cope with stress, and to become more positive in word and attitude towards others. They may want to get over problems resulting from illness, from psychological weakness or from sudden distress. Thus inner peace and developing calm are not seen as spiritual gifts but as modes and fruits of self-help. The motives of this kind of seeker are instrumental rather than spiritual. Their aim is mainly to help themselves and raja yoga can be useful in this. It is true to say that sometimes motives change during visits to the Brahma Kumari centre.

A second motive for becoming involved in the Brahma Kumaris may be an interest in various religious traditions and to visit each in turn. All religions are different and have their merits. Most teach some of the truth, yet none of them provides the whole truth. Inter-faith ministers are examples of those who can bestraddle various traditions at a time. Towards the end of the twentieth century, when New Age Movements were more common, it was possible to circulate in new religious movements while avoiding the major religious traditions. As far as Western scholarship is concerned, it is more likely that scholars who have some knowledge of the Hindu tradition will engage in research into the Brahma Kumaris. However there are other scholars, for example in the social sciences, who are able to work from their own academic background into the world-view of the Brahma Kumaris. There is also the question of what kind of research is involved. Is the scholar's interest in the Brahma Kumaris as a phenomenon and an object of research, or is it in the faith of the Brahma Kumaris as people — or is it in both? It is therefore possible for people to visit the raja-yoga centres of the Brahma Kumaris, and to gain from them, and yet to remain uncommitted to them.

The third type of attraction to the Brahma Kumaris is, so to speak, a breakaway from the second. It includes people who have roved from one religion to another in order to keep contact with various groups. After drifting for years there is a sudden sense that it is necessary to make a firm choice of one religious group — the Brahma Kumaris in this instance. Things that had been unclear and doubted before now form a pattern and arouse an intuition that makes sense.

The fourth motive outside India for becoming a Brahma Kumari may come from the experience of having had no knowledge of other religious traditions. The time is past wherein it could be guaranteed that most westerners are members of a church, or in contact with other such traditions. Thus meeting a Brahma Kumari may be someone's first awareness of spirituality or religious phenomena. They are likely to come in contact with the Brahma Kumaris via courses, which they may discover at a residential retreat, through a Inner Space centre, through community contacts or in other ways. Alternatively, someone may have come across a Brahma Kumari at their place of work or may have read some of their literature or seen them on television.

The situation in India is different. The Brahma Kumaris are present in all the state capitals and larger cities. They also live in many small cities and in some villages, and in the country as a whole there more than 850,000 regular students of the university taught in more than 8,000 centres. Now that the opposition has diminished the Brahma Kumaris are better known in India and more respected. Thus it is likely that more people will join them.

Progressive Courses

A lot of the courses run by the Brahma Kumaris World Spiritual University are geared towards encouraging people in need, while others are for people who wish to broaden their spiritual thinking and go deeper into themselves. The courses are helpful in a general sense, and they encourage visitors to grow in confidence and explore ways of improving their own lives. They are also useful socially as well, because they are free of charge. Introductory courses may be given in prisons, health situations and in places of deep need. They may also be provided in more middle class settings.

The next step may be to attend another free course on topics such as overcoming anger, positive thinking, self-esteem and stress-free living. Spiritual matters may come up in the courses as well. Feedback forms are provided for comments on courses, and the well-trained tutors have regular meetings with course co-ordinators to help them in their work.

A third course, usually but not always following the others, is a raja-yoga meditation one (see illus. 7.1). It takes as its guide a passage from the *Bhagavad Gītā* 8 verse 8:

> He who meditates on Me as the Supreme Personality of Godhead, his mind constantly engaged in remembering Me, undeviated from the path, he ... is sure to reach Me.

7.1: The Eight Powers.

This course delves more deeply into spiritual matters. Its nine modules cover:

- meditation and soul: basic steps in meditation — understanding the difference between physical and spiritual identity;
- mind, intellect and ***sanskaras***: understanding the three main faculties of the soul and how meditation can strengthen the decision-making process;
- the three worlds and introduction to God: being aware of the name, form, abode and qualities of God, and exploring a connection with God;
- the Eight Powers: how to draw power from the Supreme and use it in practical life;
- ***karma*** (including re-incarnation): awareness of the law of cause and effect and the importance of intention and motives governing action;
- the cycle of time: understanding cyclic patterns; the law of entropy; the rise and fall of human consciousness; and the relevance of the current time of transformation and transition;
- the Tree of Humanity: understanding the emergence of religions and the connectivity of souls and the Supreme;
- creation, sustenance and transformation: understanding the role of God, the Supreme Soul, in creation, sustenance and transformation;
- spiritual lifestyle: introduction to the murli and the four pillars of a spiritual lifestyle.

The course takes as its end-guide another passage from the *Bhagavad Gītā* 9 verse 2:

> This knowledge is the king of all kinds of knowledge, it is very pure, elevated and brings immediate reward, it is filled with richness, is easy to practice and imperishable. By knowing this secret of deep knowledge, persons become free from the world of sorrow.

It is clear that this course is deeper than the first two. The next step is for those who have attended the third course to start going to the morning murli sessions (if they had not done so already). The longer-run possibility is that these people would become fully fledged Brahma Kumaris and take a full part in the university in all its forms. In so doing they would have access to a worldwide community of Brahma Kumari friends and a deep spiritual life.

8

A Model of the Brahma Kumari Tradition

This chapter examimes more closely a model of the Brahma Kumaris. The model is my own and it can be applied to all religious traditions as a useful way of understanding them. It begins with a notion of transcendence, and a key medium whereby transcendence is made available to the world. In the case of the Brahma Kumaris transcendence would encompass Shiva Baba, and the medium would encompass Dada Lekhraj himself.

There are eight interlinked elements in the model: religious community; ritual; ethics; social and political involvement in wider society; concepts; aesthetics; spirituality; and scriptures and sacred texts. These elements are present in all other religious bodies in varying ways, and as far as the Brahma Kumaris are concerned all of them are (almost) there. 'Almost there' because their history is short — it covers less than a century — and it takes time to build up a tradition. Lying behind all these eight elements is the cardinal quality that holds everything together — namely faith. Faith in God (Shiva Baba) through the human medium of Brahma Baba (Dada Lekhraj) underlies everything. We will now examine in detail how this occurs.

Transcendence

Shiva Baba

The main source of transcendence is Shiva Baba, although it is important, in the first instance, to distance the Hindu ideas about the deity Shiva from the Brahma Kumari viewpoint. For Hindus Shiva is in many ways the most special Hindu deity: He is a bewildering combination of opposites (Whaling, 2010, pp. 122–5). He is the great ascetic, the incarnation of chastity and the world-renouncer, and yet His favourite symbol is the Shiva ***lingam***, which represents His male phallus. To take the contrasts within Shiva further, He is on the one hand the destroyer of the world, while on the other He is the auspicious, beneficent and gracious one who helps the world. Moreover one of His favourite symbols is of himself as Lord of the Dance, and yet He dances both the dance of bliss and the dance of destruction. Hindu devotees of Shiva revere Him from different viewpoints, in their own way and according to their own sect, their own family tradition and their own area. The great Shiva festival Mahāśivarātri takes different forms according to location.

The Brahma Kumaris view Shiva Baba totally differently. In the first place, Shiva Baba becomes active in a unique way only during the confluence age, which began in 1936 when Brahma Baba started his visions. When the confluence age is over, and a new golden age begins, Shiva Baba will return into a state of inactivity and will remain in the soul-world until the four ages of the new world cycle have run their course. At that time, He will again become active and a new confluence age will arise and a new golden age will begin. In other words, for most of the time Shiva Baba is, so to speak, an onlooker in the soul-world who allows the world on earth to go along its chosen path. When the time comes again for action He will come again to renew the world. He intervenes when the time is ripe in order to 'reveal' history at the right time.

In the second place, the Brahma Kumaris view Shiva Baba in a number of ways, but mainly as a male deity. The same is true of Brahma Baba who was not a deity but was very clearly a man. It was through him, a male, that Shiva Baba spoke to the movement. And yet, after his death, the Brahma Kumaris were led by women. And as far as they are concerned this is a satisfactory state of affairs. Part of the rationale for this is sociological change in that during the first two ages, lasting for 2,500 years, men and women had been equal. But after that there had come decline, and with that decline had come the supremacy of men. Therefore in the confluence age there was the chance for women to have their turn and to take the lead. Thus Shiva Baba is the 'supreme Father'. He loves his 'children' in a paternal way. He is masculine. He is the real father of humankind. His fatherhood is in obvious contrast to that of many earthly fathers. He wishes for women the freedom they deserve. Shiva Baba is their father in a way that gives them the autonomy to be themselves.

A third way in which the Brahma Kumaris viewpoint differs from that of Hindus is that the former see Shiva Baba as the Supreme Soul. As such He lives in the soul-world, which differs from the material world and the bodily world. In an early Brahma Kumari pictorial diagram, the universe is portrayed in the shape of an egg. At the top of the egg is the soul-world, where Shiva Baba lives, and it is surrounded by total peace and tranquillity. Bordering this world there is a red glow. At the bottom of the egg comes the material world of sound and sight and movement. This signifies where earthly life exists, and where history happens. In the middle of the egg is an in-between world called the subtle, angelic world, which is a kind of linking world between the other two. Here Brahma Baba is present, and from here murlis are sent by Bap-Dada. The key to all this is Shiva Baba, the Supreme Soul. He is pictured as a point of light. He is a point of life immersed in love. He is detached from the world of nature and history. But He is also the Father who loves his children. He is not, and cannot be, omnipresent. Yet He has all power and knowledge, and He is able to utilise them in the current confluence age.

Finally, Shiva Baba is usually portrayed as a supreme point of light. Humans also have souls that are expressed as points of light, but they are attached to bodies. However Shiva Baba is the Supreme Soul who has no attachment to a body. Inner visions of Shiva Baba are as a point of life, bathed in love. Contact with Him is through soul-contact on the part of human beings whose souls are in touch with the Supreme Soul, Shiva Baba (God). Thus Shiva Baba in the Brahma Kumari sense is not portrayed in male form, although He is male. Nor is He reproduced in human form. He is the ultimate divine soul. Contacts with Him and visions of Him take the form of the human soul as a point of light being in touch with the Supreme Soul as an unimaginably brilliant spark of incandescent light. In other words, contact with Shiva Baba is basically through meditation, not through gazing at an image or in other ways. That is why meditation, raja yoga and spirituality are so important in Brahma Kumari practice. Basically, Shiva Baba can be seen mainly as Father but also in other ways — as changeless, as an Ocean of Knowledge, as a giver of peace and happiness, as a constant source of spiritual power, as a liberator, as having no desires and even occasionally as feminine! Nor is He omnipotent. For most of the cycle of world history the immutable laws of *karma* hold sway and Shiva Baba does not infringe them. They follow their course and Shiva Baba looks on from the soul-world, where many human souls also reside, waiting to be born on to the world stage. It is only when the situation becomes desperate that Shiva Baba intervenes, although He has done so provisionally in the religious traditions of the world. At the end of the cycle, during *kali yuga*, He becomes gloriously available at the time of greatest need. He reveals himself through a mediating focus, namely Brahma Baba.

Brahma Baba

It is important to realise that Brahma Baba was not God. He was a great human leader, not a divine one. After the start of his visions people were drawn to him because of his leadership qualities, his wise counsel, his human concern, his help to the Dadis, and his know-how truly guided the movement that finally took the name of the Brahma Kumaris World Spiritual University.

It may well have been some spiritual gift of Brahma Baba that enabled others to have visions as well as himself, and indeed the visions were crucial to begin with. Later on Brahma Baba concluded that the superfluity of visions was becoming less helpful. However to a lesser extent visions continued to occur and still do so. The emphasis and concentration on spirituality allowed this to happen, and the legacy of spirituality passed on by Brahma Baba still remains.

In addition to the visions being important, they also contributed to the rise of the early murlis, which contained deep spiritual matters but moved over into practical matters as well. Many of these *sakar* murlis, given by and through by Brahma Baba while he was still alive, were lost. Fortunately, some of them were collected into book form, especially those dating from 1965 to 1969, and they are still used today in early morning sessions around the world.

For a time after Brahma Baba's death in 1969 a form of devotion (*bhakti*) to him arose among some Brahma Kumaris. It was basically worshipping him as a great and saintly man; it was not a devotion offered to him as God. According to Brahma Kumari thought Brahma Baba was translated to the intermediate subtle world where in conjunction with Shiva Baba he became Bap-Dada. In this way, Brahma Baba and Shiva Baba combine to send the murlis and to keep spiritual contact with their community.

It is now nearly fifty years since Brahma Baba passed away, and many more people have become Brahma Kumaris. By definition they have no direct earthly contact with him as had been the case with the early followers. However they see his picture every day when they go to their local centre. Therefore Brahma Baba has been and remains the key medium whereby Shiva Baba has been made available to Brahma Kumaris around the world.

Religious Community

The Brahma Kumari world network is a very close one and is mainly headed by women who bring a caring feminine element into religious leadership. It is centred in Madhuban on Mount Abu, which originally was a fairly small place. It was well organised, well led and very Indian. Impressive gigantic buildings have been built more recently and innovations to accommodate westerners and other non-Indians have been introduced, along with modern technology. Thus whereas murlis used to be sent around the world by post, they can now be distributed by email.

Madhuban is itself a unifying factor for Brahma Kumaris. Individuals and groups are encouraged to visit India, and to go to Mount Abu. It is a great adventure in more ways than one. For anyone who has lived for years in India, such a visit is more routine. For others the journey to Mount Abu is an adventure in itself. Moreover the experience of visiting Madhuban is an exciting one. For Brahma Kumaris it is equivalent to a Roman Catholic going to Rome or Lourdes, to a Sikh visiting the Golden Temple in Amritsar or to a Muslim making a pilgrimage to Mecca. The very whiteness of the Madhuban complex is redolent of the Brahma Kumari stress on purity. The day-to-day programme is helpful both to individuals and to groups. Big set-pieces, such as the receiving of the *avyakt* murlis by Dadi Gulzar, are awe-inspiring. For non-Indian visitors there is insight into some of the beauties of the place, and into the deeper practices and mysteries of the Brahma Kumari faith.

A stay at Madhuban reinforces the impression that one is part of a world family that is growing year by year. If Brahma Kumaris move around the world, there is nearly always a contact with whom they can stay and with whom the salutation *om shanti* can be shared. There are always the white-clothed sisters and brothers to look out for. Until recently brothers and sisters lived separately in all-male or all-female houses. Nowadays, for example in the Oxford Global Retreat Centre, brothers and sisters share the same building.

Most centres — central and local — organise programmes of one sort or another. In India, during Hindu festival time, some groups put on exhibitions of Brahma Kumari pictures, displayed in large tents near their centre. In tents and in local centres there may also be talks about raja yoga and the merits of spirituality as well as sound programmes of one sort or another. If the local centre is a big one it can itself be used in numerous ways, including advertising Brahma Kumari wares. For example, at the time of the Edinburgh International Festival, the local centre in Edinburgh opens its doors to host festival events and also runs raja-yoga programmes and exhibitions.

Day-by-day there are staple events at local centres. Each holds a morning meeting in which there is meditation, the murli for the day is read out and there is time for discussion and community notices. Although times and details may vary slightly from place to place, people normally arrive at the centre between 6am and 6.30am and disperse about 8am. In many centres, in the evenings, courses are held on raja yoga or other topics. Occasionally, visitors will come to speak to the group about relevant matters. Centres are therefore busy, especially if a resident sister has a local job as well.

Co-ordinating Centres

The Brahma Kumaris have a splendid network that connects all their work, and holds their people together. Each of the six world zones has a co-ordinating office that keeps in touch with all the centres in its own area. For example in the United Kingdom there are fifty-four centres, including the Oxford Global Retreat Centre and the Lighthouse Retreat Centre in Worthing. There are also Inner Space centres in Cambridge, Chelmsford, Covent Garden and Wembley (both in London) and Romford. As far as 'ordinary' centres are concerned Scotland has five centres: in Aberdeen, Dundee, Edinburgh, Glasgow and Inverness. In Ireland there are three centres: in Castlebar (County Mayo), Dublin and Galway. In Wales there are two centres: in Cardiff and Pontybodkin (Flintshire). There is one centre on the Isle of Man in Douglas. Throughout England 36 centres have been opened in 33 places: Birmingham, Brackley, Bradford, Brighton, Cambridge, Chelmsford, Colchester, Coventry, Greenford, Haverhill, Hounslow, Ilford, Kendal, Luton, Norwich, Leeds, Leicester, London (three), Loughborough, Manchester, Newcastle-on-Tyne, Nottingham, Reading, Sheffield, Slough (two), Southall, Sutton Coldfield, Tingley (Wakefield), Watford, Wellingborough, West Bromwich, Wirral and Wolverhampton.

In addition to having responsibility for all these centres in the United Kingdom, Global Co-operation House in London oversees centres in Europe and the Middle East. The same dual responsibility is held by the regional co-ordinating offices in Moscow, Nairobi, New York, Sydney and Mount Abu. Communication is made easier by computers and the internet but the Brahma Kumaris are by no means enslaved by modern technology and advanced electronics. They see themselves as a family of souls, not as a 'business'. While arranging joint conferences, dialogues, debates, discussions and colloquia at these centres, soul-friendships are created and strengthened across international boundaries as well as within national boundaries. Moreover contacts and friendships are also formed with people of other religious traditions and with secular leaders in relevant contexts.

The organisational set-up in India is more complex as there are more Brahma Kumaris there than elsewhere and languages in India differ according to region, and not everyone knows the national language of Hindi or the link language of English. As elsewhere in the world, regional groupings of centres operate in different Indian regions and states, and Mount Abu is in contact with these centres. Despite overseas expansion, the heartland of the Brahma Kumaris World Spiritual University in India, and a visit to Mount Abu remains a favoured pilgrimage for members and students from all parts of India, as well as the rest of the world. Growth of the centres in India has been spectacular and there are now thousands of them.

Types of Commitment to the Community

Within the Brahma Kumari family there are two or three kinds of attachment to the community. The main core comprises 'surrendered souls'. These can be men or women, single or married — provided they offer their lives totally to the movement and remain celibate. Such a commitment is irrevocable. Fully surrendered souls are the key members of the movement and its key workers. They are the sisters, and in some cases the brothers, who have the responsibility and honour of leading centres throughout the world. They may serve in the co-ordinating centres, which need a large dedicated band of people to work together, or they may lead single centres. If they share a celibate marriage, they may be sent to different places. They may also be vouchsafed high leadership roles such as that of Dadi or leading sister. All surrendered souls share the same food and the same mode of life. However those with leadership roles might spend more time engaged in spiritual matters, and in travelling and speaking, than the other sisters and brothers.

It is necessary to be absolutely certain about one's decision before coming fully surrendered. It requires a deep association with a centre over a period of time, and a certain amount of training to lead a centre. However other people who are surrendered may prefer to continue their jobs in the outside world, and to make regular visits to a centre. They comprise the second category of Brahma Kumaris. They attend the morning murli sessions, and are also willing to help out in other ways outside work hours.

A third category who are not totally surrendered will nevertheless be attached to a centre and have an interest in it. They may include souls who have retained their jobs and do not necessarily fully understand the underlying tenets and spirituality at the heart of the movement. But they appreciate the movement and are willing to give help.

Ceremonies and Rituals

Ritual is relatively light within the life of the Brahma Kumaris, although gathering at centres to listen to the morning murli session is a sort of ritual. The 'ceremony' begins with beautiful haunting music that provides a background to the silent meditation that is engaged in by all present. Eventually the resident sister (or in some cases the resident brother) moves forward and sits yoga-wise on a dais in the front part of the room. The music may stop at this point, and there is more silent meditation during which the sister 'gazes' at each person in turn and they gaze back at her. If the session is in a large centre with a lot of people, such as Global Co-operation House in London, this 'gazing' process takes quite a time. In some centres, important Brahma Kumari pictures displayed on the wall behind the sister are further aids to meditation. Although part of a larger audience, each person will have their own sense of making contact with Shiva Baba during this whole process.

In a clear and moving way the resident sister then delivers the morning murli for that day, and many people take notes so they can read and digest them later. The murli is a kind of analogical equivalent of a sermon delivered in a Christian church with the proviso that it is taken to be the word of God for life on that particular day. To that extent it may be more exact to compare it with a reading from the Koran, or even a Roman Catholic mass. There may be a pause in the middle of the reading, which occupies about thirty minutes to deliver. After that, there is time for questions and answers raised by the murli, followed by another short time of meditation. The people then leave quietly and return to their homes, or go to work.

There is a sense also in which the cooking of food can be seen as a kind of ritual. It is not just 'any' food. It is vegetarian food transposed, so to speak, into special food through the ritual of cooking. When it is being prepared, the cooking can be accompanied by meditation. There are, so to speak, vibrations of God in the cooking and eating of food.

Two other events, which may be added to the murli sessions, are rituals of a sort. Every third Sunday a world meditation hour is held in centres around the world. In silence, Brahma Kumaris use this time to remember the needs of the wider world as a whole, as well as those of their own immediate world. Every Thursday morning at the end of the murli session, sisters and brothers who are able to do so come forward to share in special food (***bhog***) offered in a kind of sacrament. The sister will take the *bhog* to anyone who has to remain sitting and offer it to them. The ceremony is not unlike some shortened kinds of church communion services. Furthermore, on other occasions, on Thursdays or Saturdays, people come forward to drink from a container containing nectar in a similar sacramental-type way.

Special days, such as the Ascension Day (Death Day on 18 January) of Brahma Baba and Dadi Prakashmani's equivalent day on 25 August, are remembered, and the same is true of the death days of the Dadis.

Brahma Kumaris also adapt some of the rituals of other religious traditions. This is especially true of Hindu festivals in India, which are full of joy and are sometimes rumbustious, but the Brahma Kumaris tend to quieten them down and reinterpret them.

In mid-September or early October is the Navarātri (Nine Nights) Hindu Festival, which is dedicated to the goddess Durga. The tenth night is the final and climactic time when Durga defeats a giant buffalo-demon. The Brahma Kumaris translate the festival into a peaceful event held at their own premises. At roughly the same time the famous festival of Dussehra is held, especially in north India. It is also known as Ramlila, and on the climactic night the Hindu deity Rama defeats and kills the demon Ravana. This leads to a glorious feast and celebration, especially in Banaras. This Hindu festival is much more tumultuous than the Brahma Kumari ceremony, which dwells more on the spiritual side of the whole episode.

In late October or early November the beautiful Diwali festival is held. This new year festival can be uproarious with fireworks but it can also be joyful and peaceful with majestically beautiful lights. It is easier for Brahma Kumaris to visit the quiet side of this festival as well as to arrange their own version of it.

In February, the Mahāśivarātri (Great Night of Shiva) festival commemorates Shiva's cosmic dance as Nataraja (Lord of the Dance) wherein he is both creator and destroyer of the cosmos. The Brahma Kumaris have an obvious interest in this Shiva festival but they sense that it can be interpreted as the dark night of the world that is now impending, and it is Shiva Baba rather than the Hindu deity Shiva who is heralding a new creation of the cosmos.

There is the raucous end-of-spring Holi Festival centred on Krishna in late February and the beginning of March. The Brahma Kumaris celebrate this in their own way, tending to avoid having their white clothes contaminated by coloured water.

A beautiful festival named Raksha Bandhan (Binding of Demons) occurs in August, wherein sisters bind amulets around the wrists of their brothers in order to protect them from evil. Brahma Kumari brothers and sisters have a similar moving festival, which also symbolises the union of the soul with God.

Finally, also in August, the Krishnajanmāshtamī festival celebrates the birthday of Krishna. There is singing and dancing, and special sweets are shared at midnight, the time of Krishna's birth. Again this has been adapted into Brahma Kumari modes.

In other countries too there is a similar approach to Id in Muslim areas, to the Passover in Jewish areas and to Christmas in Christian areas. In addition to adapting into Brahma Kumari terms the festivals of others, there is also a growing inter-faith awareness that makes it possible for Brahma Kumaris to take active interest in the festivals of others. However compared with the sumptuous services, the great festivals, the sacraments, the rites of passage and the exuberance of other traditions, the Brahma Kumari rituals are of less importance.

Ethics

The leading of a good life is paramount to the Brahma Kumaris, so ethics in the personal sense is important. Positively creative features need to be cultivated — for example, humility, tolerance, compassion, mercy, sweetness, cheerfulness, contentment, patience and fortitude — while negative vices that should be shed include attachment, possessiveness, arrogance, anger, greed, fear, anxiety, laziness and lust, above all sexual lust.

Brahma Kumaris generally exemplify the virtues they claim to follow. Lying behind their search for ethical wholeness is the basic drive to move from body-consciousness to soul-consciousness. The body is considered to be a wholesome instrument that must be cared for as a temporary vehicle for the soul. Vegetarian cooking done with spiritual intention is important for the sustenance of the body. Their whole spiritual regimen is seen as a psychosomatic strengthening of the resources of the body. Regular washing and bathing are recommended routines in their lives.

It is clear that basic ethical commandments, such as do not kill, do not steal, do not commit adultery, do not lie, do not bear false witness, and so on, are the central remit of the Brahma Kumaris. Their conduct has been exemplary in all these matters. They have very strong moral and ethical ideals that they have shared within their community and made available in theory to others. Their greeting *om shanti* stresses the notion and quality of peace (*shanti*), as does their non-violent philosophy towards animals.

The positive ethical virtues of non-violence, service and love are therefore built into the Brahma Kumari way of life. Although beginning as a small group that faced persecution, they later exercised positive mental attitudes to other people, viewing them as souls, and their stress on greater tolerance has led them into constructive relationships with others. It is probable that the exercise of leadership roles by women has been a beneficial factor in this respect. It has built up an ethical strength and confidence in women as women, and has brought out the nurturing ethical qualities associated with women as virtues for wider society.

The key reason that the modern advance of the Brahma Kumaris in different parts of the world has gone ahead so rapidly is that the ethic of their university has been for members to live frugally so their generosity might be of help to others. Frugality and generosity therefore are ethical Brahma Kumari bywords. While being generous to others, they live simply on vegetarian food and simple drinks. There are no visits to restaurants, cinemas, entertainments, theatres, games or other attractions that cost money. Their lifestyle is simple, and this makes it possible for them to use money in other ways. These dedicated people, who are happy to support centres financially in different ways, enable the work of the Brahma Kumaris to prosper. A number of sisters or brothers who run and live in centres give their services free of charge and have paid jobs during the day, and the payments they receive are of help to their own community. Even in the large London centre some people have an outside day job and work in the centre at night. Therefore apart from costs such as electricity and taxes the work of a centre can proceed without undue financial pressure. There are however donation boxes in centres but they are not highlighted in any obvious way. Recently, students who take courses have the opportunity to make a donation, but it is not obligatory.

The ethic of purity at the heart of the movement has been encouraged by its sociological background, which had exploited the issue of vulnerable sexuality. It was also aided by the murlis, which opened up a new way of life. As the *The Story of Immortality: A Return to Self-Sovereignty* puts it:

> The story of souls in time is a story of the loss of our original greatness and eventually even the forgetting that we were great, until one day — utterly disoriented and on the brink of despair — we are lucky enough to find a hidden door that takes us on to a path of ascent that was invisible before. Today the world is filled with people wandering in search of something — some are searching for truth, some are searching for God. Always it is a search for a new identity — an explanation of who they really are and where they fit into the vast story of humanity. This is the story of the confluence age, the most subtle and elevated of the great ages of humankind. However unlike the other ages, this one is available only to those who grasp the difference between the temporal, material world and the eternal, spiritual universe that moves within it (Panjabi and Janki, 2008, book cover).

The authors go on to state:

> Those who know the Brahma Kumaris may know them for wearing white, for the fact that they are led by women, for their practice of open-eyed meditation, for their emphasis on self-transformation, or for the greeting of 'om shanti'. They do not

> chant. They have a minimal number of rituals. And they have a practice of raja-yoga meditation that involves self-transformation through elevated thoughts and connection with the divine in silence.
>
> What most people don't know about the Brahma Kumaris is the base of knowledge that constitutes their foundation. Raja yoga, the oldest meditation and the newest, is not a devotional path. It is a path of lifelong learning, study, and application in daily life. Until now, the foundational knowledge of the Brahma Kumaris has been available primarily through a course given orally from one person to another. Because they understand this knowledge to be so vital for the world at this time, the Brahma Kumaris have undertaken to share it more broadly in this book (Panjabi and Janki, 2008, frontispiece).

This important statement represents a kind of coming-of-age. It means that the original questions, raised by Brahma Baba through the murlis with a tiny community that had seen purity and other things as internal matters, were now part of a global agenda that was relevant to all. Answers are now conveyed not only by word of mouth in local centres by local people, important as that is, but also by global figures, and global books, in global ways. There is now the opportunity for the Brahma Kumaris to be more involved within wider society, and to have a clearer and more informed impact on a wider audience, as their remit (including purity) becomes more widely seen and known.

Social and Political Involvement in Wider Society

The fourth element in the eightfold pattern of the model focuses on social and political involvement in wider society. The Brahma Kumaris have little interest in the politics of any country or party, although they have been happy, more recently, to engage with political leaders in order to be of help in spiritual and ethical ways with a view to giving assistance to those in need.

Although initially — while in Hyderabad and Karachi — the Brahma Kumaris had no particular commitment to social problems, the Brahma Kumaris World Spiritual University is now engaged in a number of areas of life in a caring way. The word 'spiritual' is a key word in their self-description. Their fellowship in the university is of a friendly, supportive and caring nature but it is basically spiritual. Good relationships have been set up with the United Nations wherein the Brahma Kumaris are a valued group. Helpful support has also been given to some parliaments, and also to prisons, hospitals, schools and other institutions. But the motive behind this support has been humane and spiritual rather than political in nature. They are very good at giving hospitality to others, but gently prefer not to receive it themselves.

At the level of promoting good works, and setting up programmes that can aid others, the Brahma Kumaris are devoted helpers of all those who seek their succour and support and they finance this work themselves. They are now increasingly concerned about the number of people requiring help in different parts of the world, so their involvement has gone beyond the realms of spirituality into a much wider range of activities. In her short statement about the building of Diamond House to enable the work of Global Co-operation House in London to blossom Dadi Janki writes:

> Now Global Co-operation House has become too small, and Diamond House has been built to provide a conference hall, more office space, a larger meditation room and children's facilities. It is a great step forward. I am deeply grateful to the London Borough of Brent and to all helpers and well-wishers who have made it possible (BKWSU, n.d., p. 4).

This is a remarkable statement from someone who suffered an enforced marriage, had a child against her will and underwent a series of traumatic moves from Hyderabad to Karachi, then from Karachi to Mount Abu, and then out into wider India, before arriving in London. It demonstrates the extraordinary evolution of Dadi Janki's vision from the enclosed situation in Hyderabad to the blossoming possibilities in London — not only for spiritual growth but also for wider community expansion alongside. As Dadi Prakashmani writes, also in connection with the opening of Diamond House:

> Actions filled with love inspire co-operation in any task. Being filled with love, we have inner strength and will never do anything that diminishes our own dignity or that of another. When we are filled with God's love — it is natural to share it abundantly. By giving love without conditions, we receive blessing beyond measure (BKWSU, n.d., pp. 4–5).

There has been space to mention only some of the work that is being done with other groups and with other areas of life in many parts of the world. It is important also to remember that the Brahma Kumaris provide their own money to engender these various kinds of work.

Concepts or Beliefs

All religious groups have a set of concepts that are important to them. In the case of the Brahma Kumaris the murlis that were spoken by Brahma Baba while alive, and by Dadi Gulzar after his demise, form the main basis for the conceptual background to their faith. Also essential are the lessons taught in centres. It is helpful to summarise the main concepts of the Brahma Kumaris World Spiritual University in some sort of intellectual order in order to understand them as an underlying system of ideas.

Concepts for their own sake, in the sense of theologically normative ideas, are not central to the university's consciousness, and in this they resonate with their Hindu background. However the category of 'knowledge' is important for the Brahma Kumaris, as spirituality is related to knowledge. It does not exist in a vacuum. They are two sides of the same coin. Therefore concepts in the sense of 'knowledge' are very significant for this spiritual university, which has no vice-chancellors, professors, lecturers or students. It does not have university terms, not does it have celebrities who are paid vast salaries. It does stress knowledge, but it is knowledge in the sense of ***gyan***. Such knowledge includes spiritual knowledge as a central part of its teaching.

The sources of Brahma Kumari knowledge are mainly twofold: a vastly modified version of aspects of the Hindu world-view; and the visions vouchsafed to Brahma Baba. The importance of those visions, when interpreted, give them a similar status to that of 'revealed knowledge' in other traditions. There is however the caveat that this 'revealed knowledge' is linked to spirituality, and it becomes truly meaningful only when it becomes alive spiritually.

A third important aspect of Brahma Kumari knowledge, and of all other features of their life, is not obviously present in either the Hindu world-view or in Brahma Baba's visions. It is the centrality of women in the ethos and leadership of the movement. Yet this subtly influences the way in which knowledge is given, received and shared.

Beginner's Curriculum

What then are the main ingredients of the university's concepts? The university's own distillation of the essence of its knowledge appears in the seven lessons contained in the course taken by newcomers in its earlier years.

The first lesson outlines the crucial importance of the soul and its distinction from the body. The soul is, so to speak, the driver within the vehicle of the body. In practice, some people argue that it is the body that dominates or even 'writes off' the soul. But this is to misunderstand the relationship, and to put the cart before the horse. The role of the soul is crucial. It is the essential instrument rather than the body. The soul, it is said, has three separate faculties: the mind, the intellect and the *sanskaras* (impressions). Thoughts are originally created in the mind, and they are the basis of our emotions, desires and sensations. It is therefore necessary to control the mind in order to harmonise one's thoughts and sensations. The second faculty of the soul, the intellect, is used to assess thoughts. Its understanding is subtle and spiritual, and is not to be equated with the brain. Therefore through the spiritual university the mind is controlled and the intellect is developed and elevated. The *sanskaras* are the personality traits built up within a person as a result of the actions done in this life and in past lives. They have a strong pull in the direction of bodily interests and away from the soul. Through the work of the spiritual university unhelpful *sanskaras* can be purified and helpful *sanskaras* strengthened.

The second lesson focuses on God the supreme. Of the three worlds connected with the notion of Shiva Baba as God, the physical one in which we live is known as the corporeal world of matter and physical elements. It is the world where humans live. The second world is the subtle world of light and it is sometimes known as the astral plane. This is an intermediate world where Brahma Baba lives and from which Bap-Dada communicates the murlis to the physical world. Beyond the subtle world is the incorporeal or supreme world where stability, peace and silence reign. It is the home of God, and it is also the world from which all souls come and to which they will all ultimately go, at any rate for a short time. This concept of the three worlds feeds into Brahma Kumari meditation, which allows them to go from the physical world to the supreme world where Shiva Baba resides, and to experience deep peace there.

The third lesson elaborates further on the notion of the three worlds and explains in more depth how by means of raja yoga a deep spirituality can be experienced. The concept of raja yoga is very important to the Brahma Kumaris, and for some years they were known in some quarters, and especially in the West, as the raja-yoga movement. Content-wise within Hinduism, raja yoga subsumes, synthesises and modifies six kinds of yoga found in the Hindu tradition: hatha yoga is based on determination and discipline; bhakti yoga on love and devotion; *karma* yoga on pure action in the world; sannyasa yoga on renunciation; buddhi yoga on depth of understanding; and jnana yoga on knowledge. As far as the Brahma Kumaris are concerned there is some stress on spiritual experience in their understanding and practice of raja yoga, and some elements of raja yoga are clearly related to concepts and knowledge.

The fourth lesson at the Brahma Kumaris World Spiritual University discourses on the notion of *karma*, which means work or actions. According to this concept each person is responsible for their actions. All of these have their consequences, and each person sows what they reap. If their *karma* is good there will be good results, if their *karma* is not good there will be adverse ones. According to the Brahma Kumaris there are three kinds of *karma*. The first, *vikarma*, is negative action that produces sorrow, and that comes through the practice of vices connected with body-consciousness, namely lust, anger, greed, attachment and ego. The second kind, *sukarma*, is positive and pure action that produces happiness and which occurs through practice of the virtues connected with soul-consciousness. The third kind, *akarma*, is neither positive or negative. It is neutral in its effects and has to do with things such as sleeping and sustaining the body. The claim is that by understanding the concept of *karma* and through an ongoing link with God everyone can be freed from future bad *karma* and from the *karma* built up in past births, and they can build up a store of good *karma,* which will be helpful in the future.

The fifth lesson outlines the university view of the cosmic cycle. This is rooted in eternity and will have no end. However in human consciousness, world history repeats itself in a cosmic drama involving four ages: the golden, silver, copper and iron ages. These last for 1,250 years each, giving a cosmic cycle of 5,000 years. The golden age, and to a lesser extent the silver age, are a time of paradise on earth when civilisation, culture, earthly beauty and ecological sufficiency are at their zenith. Souls who have built up spiritual power through raja yoga or in other ways will have the benefit of living in this earthly paradise, this garden of Eden. Roughly a million souls are involved at the beginning of the golden age and the number slowly increases through the silver age, while at the same time the quality of life in paradise slowly dilutes. At the end of the silver age there is what amounts to a fall from soul-consciousness, which has dominated the golden and silver ages, into body-consciousness. The world turns into the world that is now familiar, and physical awareness begins to dominate human consciousness. This process of decline continues through the copper and iron ages until the nadir at the end of *kali yuga* (iron age). At this point God intervenes directly to change an unhelpful situation by descending into Brahma Baba, and during the confluence age that ensues *kali yuga* continues towards its denouement and a new golden age is anticipated with the cosmic drama, the eternal cycle, beginning again. If someone is born at the start of the golden age they will experience eighty-four births in all throughout the 5,000 year cycle. Otherwise, they will wait quiescently in the silent world until their turn to descend has arrived.

The sixth lesson elaborates on the role played by Brahma Baba in the cosmic drama as one into whom God descends in order to effect the coming transformation, and as the one who, together with Om Radhe, offers beneficent and caring leadership at the approach of the golden age.

The seventh and final lesson elaborates on the notion of the eternal world tree. It spells out the part that is played by religions and civilisations in the copper and iron ages. The main religions of the world appeared at that time of decline, and yet are fundamental in their own right. Inter-faith dialogue has become important for the Brahma Kumaris, and the religious traditions and leaders of the world (especially Krishna and Christ) are highly regarded. Indeed in recent lessons other religious leaders, including a Hindu *Shankaracharya*, Guru Nanak and Muhammad, have been added to Abraham, Christ and the Buddha as crucial leaders. Moreover the Brahma Kumaris agree that names for the golden age are mentioned by other traditions: for example, the Garden of Eden by Jews and Christians; the Garden of Allah by Muslims; Vaikunth by Hindus; the Field of Osiris by Egyptians; the Dreamtime of the Australian Aborigines; the Heaven of Warriors by the Aztecs; Mount Olympus by the Greeks; and Land of the Ever Young by the Celtics. Nevertheless, attempts by other religions to solve the world's problems would appear to be in vain. The Brahma Kumaris agree that inter-faith co-operation is a splendid thing but it is not able to stave off the coming end of the world.

The Concept of Knowledge

The body of knowledge summarised above borrows from, yet radically alters, Hindu concepts: for example, the aeons of time involved in the Hindu *yugas* are telescoped into 5,000 years. The Hindu notion that knowledge is linked to spiritual realisation is also prominent. Yet the emphasis is ultimately placed not so much on escaping from the round of rebirths into spiritual ***moksha*** (**nirvana**), but on being born again immediately into a paradise on earth. It is the network of ideas that is important even though the body of knowledge is in a sense ancillary to spirituality, because it is revealed knowledge — knowledge given directly by God to Brahma Baba. In other words, the substance of and the attitude to knowledge within the spiritual university is both similar to and different from the mainstream Hindu tradition.

The university may have originated and grown in India but from about 1969 its remit was worldwide. Thus a welter of new projects are no longer

British, or American, or African, or so on. They are global projects that happen to be taking part in particular countries. They are matters of global concern. A parallel attempt has been made to use local languages and turns of phrase to explain the meaning of Indian or Hindu terms in local vernaculars.

The seven-lesson course presented to beginners has since been increased to nine lessons and taught in vernacular forms, which make it easier for students around the world to learn more quickly.

If the university is becoming more global, so also is the context of its murlis. The early ones arose from an unusual situation that related to Sind in a particular part of India. They were received in that situation, which was unique. Most of them have disappeared and the ones used now date mainly from the period 1965–9, although some of these *sakar* murlis reflect the background of the time. The *avyakt* murlis received through Dadi Gulzar as trance medium have as their background later issues that can be discussed in an evolving way.

It is significant that a lot of recent literature has expanded the murli themes: for example, a series of books on practical spirituality for better living gives insights and experiences derived from knowledge about and practice of raja-yoga meditation. The books inevitably contain a lot of material about the concepts of the university, and other matters to do with the university. Twelve of them focus on self-development; eleven on higher consciousness; ten on elements of spirituality and well-being; six are children's books; and five are vegetarian cookbooks. The series has been compiled by Brahma Kumari Publications, the literature division of the Brahma Kumaris Publications Information Services Limited, in association with the Brahma Kumaris World Spiritual University. Any profits from sales are covenanted in order to further the charitable activities of the university. In addition, an award-winning set of Living Values books enables parents and teachers to develop and enhance twelve critical social values for young people in an educational programme. Other books and sources of learning criss-crossing the boundaries between concepts, social involvement and spirituality add to the wealth of information and learning, both theoretical and practical, that is emanating from the university. The Brahma Kumari Publications catalogue, for example, includes four audio CDs on creative meditation, four on relaxation commentaries, ten on informative talks, sixteen on relaxation music, eight on inspirational songs and eight on meditations for children. There are also eleven CDs, including one narrrated by Dawn French (of *Vicar of Dibley* fame), called 'Chasing God'.

Aesthetics

The sixth element in the model is that of aesthetics. Again, because of their relative newness, it is too soon for the Brahma Kumaris to have produced significant art, sculpture, music and architecture — the equivalents of great cathedrals or the Taj Mahal. However they do have a strong cultural interest.

Female and many male members of the movement wear white clothing as a sign of purity, although such clothing is also worn as a matter of aesthetic neatness. It is an outward sign of being a Brahma Kumari (woman) or Brahma Kumar (man).

Parallel to the whiteness of attire has been a fascinating use of white buildings in different places around the world. Their utilitarian buildings exude an attractiveness of their own, partly because of the appealing whiteness of their exteriors — such structures, so to speak, representing architectural purity. The buildings at Madhuban on Mount Abu are typical. Because of their whiteness they stand out from the multi-coloured 'chaos' of other Indian buildings on the mountain. In addition to white buildings that kindle notions of purity, the Brahma Kumaris have also purchased buildings such as the Oxford Global Retreat Centre that are not white, so they have amended them in other aesthetic ways.

Sensitive use of music is another important aesthetic hallmark: for example, appropriate music is played at murli sessions. Gifted Brahma Kumaris often give their services to record music for use by their fellows, and occasionally professionals are recruited to record music for a special programme or celebration. The music concerned is evocative, haunting and moving. Some of it has similarities with a certain kind of New Age music, although Brahma Kumaris are keen to stress that they are not part of the New Age movement.

Another manifestation of aesthetics is the beauty of many unusual and extraordinary pictures on display in Brahma Kumari buildings. They may be used as favoured objects of contemplation, and be spiritually elevating. Although the emphasis is on spirituality, they often illustrate and demonstrate aesthetic effectiveness as well. Some paintings hang in all Brahma Kumari centres, while a greater number of important ones are displayed in larger centres. The paintings often include one of Brahma Baba himself, along with a photograph of him. There may also be his original visions put into picture form. Thus they may show an interpretation of the original vision of the Hindu deity Vishnu whereby Brahma Baba had sensed that he was being called to special work. The paintings will also include a vision of the future golden age as a paradise of beauty that will return again and become available again, as well as some portraying figures of Hindu deities who might be around in the golden age. Displayed too will be a picture of the three worlds (the material world, the subtle world and the soul-world) (see illus. 4.1, p. 45) and one of Brahma Baba's sombre vision of destruction involving explosions and crumbling buildings. In addition to these original paintings, others that appeared later in Karachi included images of Om Radhe (and other Dadis), the world cycle and the tree of humanity, depicting the emergence of the different world religions (see illus. 4.2, p. 46).

Spirituality

The seventh element is that of spirituality, and this is arguably the deepest foundation of Brahma Kumari life. It is central and vital and may well be the most important element of all within the Brahma Kumaris World Spiritual University — as indeed the designation spiritual university suggests. It is the outstanding treasure among the eight elements that sum up the being of each Brahma Kumari, whose aim is to cultivate a total God-consciousness. The key to their life is spirituality. A number of them meditate at around 4am every morning for roughly three-quarters of an hour on the themes of 'Who am I?' — the answer being that each person is a pure soul; on God to whom they 'fly' metaphorically to be with him in the supreme world; and on behalf of the world to which they send vibrations of spiritual concern before they go out to be of service to the world. In addition to meditation at the 6.30am murli session, and during the evening meditation session, Brahma Kumaris try to remember God every hour on the hour. That happens mainly in centres where music sounds the advent of each hour, and people stop for two minutes to meditate. Their spirituality is vibrant and effective.

A flavour of the nature of their meditation is evident at the end of the former first lesson of their course:

> Turn your thoughts, your mind, to the self, the real I, the soul, a point of light ... I, the soul, am a point of light ... a tiny point of energy ... I sit in the centre of my forehead — This is the real I ... the real me ... my physical body is but a costume ... which I, the living energy, use ... it exists for me to express my being ... through which to express my personality ...
>
> Now I realise my true identity ... I have unlocked my prison door ... I am now free ... like a bird, I can fly again ...
>
> I now emerge my true nature, that of peace ... I experience that peace ... I become that peace ... I am that peace ... I experience

> my true nature ... that of light ... I become that light ... I am that light ... I experience my true nature ... that of love ... I become that love ... I am that love ...
>
> Now power is being filled in the soul ... lightness and ease become my nature ... now no longer am I the slave but the master of this body ... I spread the light and purity into the world.

Raja Yoga

The object of raja-yoga meditation is to achieve communication with God — it is not just a concentration exercise. Raja yoga therefore involves the experience of union with God, which includes familiarity with peace, love, bliss and power, and during daily life and work the aim is to practise union with God in each person and to radiate it out to others.

A meditating Brahma Kumari sits at ease, or squats in the lotus position or in one that is comfortable. Meditation is done with the eyes open. At the first stage of raja yoga the mind is used actively, and if the mind races this is allowed to happen. But the direction in which the mind is going is controlled by the intellect, which focuses on questions such as: What am I? What are my real qualities? What is my real nature? Where is my real home? Who is my Father? Who is God? What is my relation to Him? What are His qualities?

The soul ponders these questions, and as it finds and deepens the answers it moves away from the corporeal world into the subtle one where meditation is natural. There is full concentration on God and there is a sense of going deeper into the ocean of God. Conscious thoughts are still the order of the day, but they are now focused on God rather than other areas of spiritual knowledge. The soul speaks to God and thoughts become calmer and quieter. As the mind becomes still each meditator hears what God is saying. There is an experience of God as he is. An experience of the qualities of God floods into the soul, which absorbs them and is transformed, and in turn the soul begins to radiate these qualities into the world. A stage is reached where there are no longer conscious thoughts at work. Pure experience has taken over. The Brahma Kumaris then take this God-consciousness into their daily lives and live it out as a vehicle of change in the world.

Strictly speaking there are four components within raja yoga as taught by the Brahma Kumaris. The first is that of knowledge, which is imparted and received in order to be able to pass on into the realm of meditation in its own right. Secondly, meditation or remembrance within raja yoga can be done either at home alone, or as part of the murli sessions. It involves moving inward, being silent, 'remembering' God, experiencing peace and being soul-conscious. It means relating to God, and experiencing God as Father, teacher, friend, counsellor and even mother. This meditational relationship with God is of deep importance personally, and the spiritual attainments it offers are spurs to go out and engage in service to others. A third component within raja yoga covers the practice of inculcating personal knowledge and experience into daily life in order to help others. This may involve each person filling in an ongoing chart or diary so that they can deepen their awareness of God and creatively monitor their daily actions. This was what the early Puritans did; moreover, they also stopped work hourly to remember God. The final component within raja yoga is actually going out to assist others. This can entail serving them via the mind, through spoken words or by actions of one sort or another. It can even involve using all three forms of service separately or together. Good actions in time of need should be drawn from one of the eight powers recommended in a university lesson. They are the powers to withdraw, tolerate, co-operate, accommodate, discern, decide, face something and pack up.

Scripture and Sacred Texts

The eighth and last element in the model is that of scripture and sacred texts. At the moment these are not present for the Brahma Kumaris in the obvious sense of those words. The history of most religious traditions shows that it takes time for scriptures to be set down and identified. The Brahma Kumari equivalents to scripture and sacred texts are still in the making: they are the murlis that have been read out and handed down over the years.

A Complete 1980 Murli

Here is a murli spoken on 4 January 1980, at Madhuban: 'The One who has claimed the rights of self-sovereignty in the present can claim the rights of sovereignty in the future':

> Do you all consider yourselves to have claimed the right to double-sovereignty? To have the rights of sovereignty over the present is to have the rights of sovereignty in the future also. The present is the mirror of the future. You can see your future very clearly through the mirror of your present stage. In order to keep the rights of sovereignty over the present and over the future, always check this: to what extent is ruling power contained within the self? First of all, to what extent have you

claimed rights over your subtle powers which perform special work for you; to what extent do you reign over your power of thought, intellect and innate tendencies (*sanskaras*)? Once you have claimed sovereignty over these special three powers, they will give constant co-operation. They are the main helpers in the work of administering your kingdom (of the self). If these three helpers perform according to the signal of you the soul, you the king, who has claimed the right to sovereignty, then your kingdom will always run accurately, just as the Father also gets His work done through the trinity. That is why the trinity is highly praised and worshipped. They do speak of Trinity Shiva. The One Father has three special workers through whom He has the work of the whole world done. Similarly, you souls are also creators and these three special powers, the trinity powers, are your special workers. You are also the creators of these three creations. So check whether you have control over this trinity creation.

The mind is the creator; it creates thoughts. The intellect is for judging and so does work comparable to sustenance. The *sanskaras* are for transforming the good from the bad. Just as Brahma is the first created man (Adi Dev), so also the first power is the mind, that is the power of thought. If that first power is accurate, then the other workers, its many companions, will also work accurately. So first check this: does the very first worker always, like a close companion, act on the signal of me, the king? Because Maya, the enemy, also first of all makes this original power into a renegade and traitor and tries to take over your right to the kingdom. That is why on the basis of your authority make this first power your right and true helper, and make it perform its special work, just as the king does not do any task himself, but he gets it done through others, and the ones who actually do the work are separate from the king's ministers. If the king's ministers are not accurate, then the kingdom begins to shake. In the same way, the soul is the one who gets things done, and the doers are these special trinity powers.

First of all, if you have ruling powers over these three, then on that basis the physical sense organs will automatically take the right path. These three special powers are the very ones that make the sense organs work. Now, how far have you achieved this ruling power? Check this.

Just as you are double foreigners (your native land being the soul-world), are you also double rulers? Is the administration of each one's kingdom in order, that is to say, is each one's self-sovereignty proceeding accurately? Just as for the golden aged world it is said that there is one kingdom and one religion, in the same way now also, in this self-sovereignty, there should be one rule; everything should be going ahead from a mere signal. One religion means that everyone is united in their inculcation to do everything in an ever elevated way and be in the rising degree.

If your mind becomes wilful, disturbing the judgement power of the intellect thereby creating confusion, and if the *sanskaras* are making the soul dance to their own tune, this could not be called unity of religion, unity in the kingdom. So how is your kingdom? Are the trinity powers all right? Or do the *sanskaras* sometimes make you dance like a monkey? What do monkeys do? They jump up and down and cavort around, don't they? The *sanskaras* also sometimes bring you in the rising degree and sometimes in the declining degree. So I hope that *sanskaras* don't make you jump in this way. You all have control, don't you? Your intellect doesn't sometimes get confused, does it? Just as nowadays they confuse people, and their power of judgement becomes clouded, so I hope your intellect doesn't sometimes become confused. If your judgement is sometimes correct and sometimes wasted, it means there is confusion (Chander, 1983b, pp. 276–8).

Key Murli Themes

The following miscellany of extracts from countless murlis on basic matters bring together twelve of the key themes within the whole ongoing movement. They not only give an insight into the murlis themselves but also summarise through the murlis the essence of the Brahma Kumari tradition. Insofar as they are brought together from many different murlis, and the wording has been changed for simplicity's sake, they are of necessity not verbatim or quotations as such.

Soul

A soul is truly a star. Many of those are visible. A soul is a point of light. There are as many souls as there are human beings. The body of a person is visible with these eyes but the soul can only be seen with divine vision.

People have different features, but souls are not different; all are the same. It is just that the role of every soul is different. Human beings are big or small whereas souls are not bigger or smaller. The size of souls is the same.

All souls are eternal and imperishable. All souls have received their own body, their own parts (to play), on this world stage. Originally the soul is a resident of the land of silence.

God

The Father says: I am the seed of the human world, the truth, the Living Consciousness, the Embodiment of Bliss, the Ocean of Knowledge, the Ocean of Peace and the Ocean of Love, the Lord of the Tree, the Purifier of all. I make the old world new. I am the creator of heaven. All the virtues are in Him. The most beloved is the Father.

Only God, the Supreme Soul, is incorporeal and egoless. Only God, the Father, can give His children such altruistic love. He does not enter the cycle of birth and death. He does not have His own body. He is a point of light.

Only the One Father is the liberator of all. The Father himself comes at the time of sorrow to liberate you from ***ravan*** (vices) and He then becomes your guide and takes you back home. He is called the spiritual guide. The Father says: I am the guide of all of you souls. I will take all of you back home. There is no other guide like Me. People say: God, the Father, is the liberator, the guide, the Blissful One.

Mind, Intellect, Sanskars

The mind, intellect and ***sanskars*** (personality traits) are three faculties of the soul. However it requires subtle practice to become victorious over the subtle powers of the mind, intellect and *sanskaras.*

For the mind, there is churning (reflective) power for words and actions, there is the power to tolerate in order to create positive thoughts in your mind. If you have the power to tolerate, whatever you think, words you speak and actions you perform will be pure and successful. This is also called controlling power. So all three spiritual powers are essential.

It is especially the mind that causes obstacles. Become a master of the mind, never be influenced by the mind. Just see: in any little wasteful incident, or wasteful atmosphere, or wasteful scene, where is the first influence felt? There is the influence of the mind, so that within a second the mind has bad feelings over a little incident. The intellect then co-operates with it, and if mind and intellect move in that direction, it becomes a *sanskar.*

Meditation

Meditation is to stabilise yourself in your original stage (to consider yourself a soul) and you will then experience your qualities and virtues. Soul-consciousness means remembrance of the Father (God).

Meditation is to focus the mind and intellect on God. It is only then that you can stabilise yourself in an elevated stage, and spread the waves of co-operation and the light and might of good wishes and pure feelings to the world.

Meditation is to practise controlling all your waste thoughts within a second. Throughout the day, move along in waves of pure thoughts, and go to the bottom of the ocean of good thoughts, and become the embodiment of silence when you want,

This means that your brake should be fully powerful. You should be able to control the power of your mind. As well as this power, the other two powers of your soul, your intellect and *sanskars*, all three powers should be under the control of you, the soul.

Spiritual Lifestyle

'Brahmin' in the Brahma Kumari sense stands for one who has taken a spiritual rebirth, it does not stand for the Brahmin caste in the Hindu sense.

Brahmin life has four main foundations. Brahmins are those who study and teach others God's knowledge. Brahmin life means a godly student life. The four main subjects of study are the main foundations of Brahmin life: One who has understanding and knowledge of God; an easy Raja Yogi; One who has divine virtues (spiritual qualities); and a world server (altruistic).

The special qualification of someone who has knowledge of God is to experience the stage of being loving and detached in every thought, word, action and connection.

Purity does not just mean celibacy. Complete purity means that none of the vices should be touched even in thought.

World Transformation

World transformation is the special task of Brahmin life, just as the Father, the creator of the world, is instrumental in transforming the world. Those who transform the world, first of all have to transform themselves. By transforming their awareness in one second, and stabilising in the awareness of the soul not the body, then it is possible to: 1) Transform your awareness in one second. 2) Transform your attitude in one second. 3) Transform your nature and *sanskars* (negative traits) in one second. 4) Transform your thoughts.

Confluence Age

The confluence age is the land of happiness and benevolence. It is the age to have all attainments (virtues) for always and to become elevated and make others elevated. It is between the iron age and golden age. Then clouds of sorrow and unhappy incidents come to an end for those who see Brahmins' happiness: they forget their sorrow and begin to swing in the swing of happiness.

The power of truth makes the whole of nature ***satopradhan*** (pure). It makes all souls attain the fortune of their salvation. With the power of truth given by the true Father, all souls will incarnate into their own religion, at their own time and in their own capacity, from liberation into salvation.

World Cycle

For half the cycle (golden and silver ages) there is pure sustenance and a pure world. Truly there was plenty of happiness. In the golden age the deities (people) of Bharat had divine intellects. Five thousand years ago this Bharat was the land of divinity (heaven) where deities used to reside. Bharat is remembered as the imperishable land. There were no other lands.

So for half the cycle you were born through purity and you were full of virtues (purity, peace, love). Impurity was finished. This completion is called the complete stage. A successful ***tapaswi*** (yogi) means that the personality and royalty of purity should automatically be experienced in your every word, every action and through your vision and attitude.

For the other half of the cycle (copper and iron ages) you continued to come down the ladder and the omens continued to change. Souls are now being influenced by the many types of bondage, sorrow and lack of peace. They are influenced by suffering through their body, influenced by relations, by desires, by sorrows of their sorrowful *sanskars* and natures, by the sorrow of not finding God, and by wandering and stumbling through lack of peace. Some are distressed by not having a clear aim in life. This is called the predestined eternal world drama. Originally, the soul is a resident of the land of silence. All souls are eternal and imperishable, all souls have received their own body and their own parts to play. This world is a theatre.

Karma Philosophy

If you are controlled by your actions, that is if you are controlled by the desires of the perishable fruit of *karma* (action), then that *karma* will tie you in bondage and continue to make your intellect wander. That is called the bondage of ***karma*** that causes distress for the self and others too. ***Karmateet*** means someone who is not dependent on *karma*, but someone who comes into a relationship (connection) with the physical senses as their master, as an authority, someone who is detached from perishable desires and makes the physical senses act. Thus *karma* should not make the soul, the master, dependent but as one with rights. He should enable the senses to continue to perform actions. When physical senses attract you, it means that you are controlled by your actions. You remain dependent and tied.

It is the task of the eyes to see, but who is it that enables the eyes to see? The eyes perform the action, but it is the soul that enables that action to be performed. So when the soul that makes an action be performed becomes dependent on the physical senses that perform the action that is called the bondage of *karma*.

When you become one who makes actions be performed or makes an action take place, it is called coming into relationship with *karma*. A *karmateet* soul comes into relationship, but does not remain tied in bondage.

The Three Worlds

The entire physical world is the corporeal world (Earth) where there is sound and movement. Human beings (embodied souls) reside here. The body is created out of five elements. Souls come here to play their part. All the souls who are here are actors in this drama.

In the subtle (angelic) region, you can meet Baba (the Father) whenever you want, for as long as you want. However many want to meet Baba can do so because it is beyond the world of limits. There is no sound in the subtle region.

Shiva Baba (the Supreme Soul) resides in the soul-world with incorporeal souls, in the land of peace. That is the great dimension of light. The One resides beyond in the supreme abode, the land beyond sound and the land of silence.

The Eight Spiritual Powers

In order to become a practical embodiment of all virtues, it is necessary to receive all the powers from the Father, such as the power to withdraw, the power to pack up waste thoughts, the power to tolerate, the power to accommodate, the power to discern, the power to decide, the power to face, the power to co-operate.

The virtue is to put all the powers into practice to make difficult things easy and bring about transformation. The main area for Brahmins is to stabilise the intellect, so that you are then constantly able to stabilise yourself in that place. You can also stay in that stage while walking and moving around. The essence of all aspects is included in this. Of course all things would be included in the expansion, but merge the expansion into one word. The place of residence means the stage in which you stabilise yourself, and that is as a detached observer. When you do not have the stage of a detached observer, you then forget all these things. In order to stay on the track of the drama, and to perform every action and have every thought while holding the shield of the drama, let the stage remain of being detached while interacting and being a detached observer.

Discernment

Discernment is the practice of being able to discern the present and the future in any situation and in connection with souls with any kind of thoughts. In order to face different situations, cleanliness of the intellect is absolutely essential.

Those whose intellects are solely engaged in remembrance of the One (God), and are in the stage of soul-consciousness, are essential. However together with the stage of soul-consciousness, only those who do not have a lot of waste thoughts, and are able accurately to discern the thoughts, words and actions of other souls, can recognise others as they are. Those whose intellects create a lot of thoughts will have a mixture of their own waste thoughts in understanding others.

No matter how clever someone may be, there is a great difference in being able to discern and decide when the intellect is tired by these waste thoughts throughout the day. It lacks the power to make decisions, and is therefore not able to become victorious.

Faith

The final link in the model of the Brahma Kumaris is the basic ingredient of human faith or human intention, which gives life to the above-mentioned eight elements, and makes transcendence real. This is crucial and dictates the quality of faith, not in the Protestant sense of a Luther or a Karl Barth, but as that which gives an understandable pattern to life. In many Brahma Kumari spiritual biographies there is a sense of coming home when the writer discovers the spiritual university, of feeling that life added up to a whole, and that they had found their true self.

Brahma Kumari faith is a strong phenomenon even though the faith of individuals may grow or decline in intensity. It is not a passing phase, as is sometimes the case among major religions where a number of people are born into a tradition that means little to them and has little or no rooting in their lives. For a Brahma Kumari, the new faith even initially involved sacrifice and possible persecution. It meant leaving home and embarking on a new lifestyle. Even though things have changed since then, joining the Brahma Kumaris World Spiritual University still connotes sacrifice. It means a lifelong spiritual commitment. It embraces self-sacrifice in regard to monetary and other perks of life in the world. It denotes an ongoing concern for others. Surrendered souls are surrendered for life.

Because the eight elements in the model are intertwined, a dilemma with one of them may have repercussions with one or two of the others. Thus, although many more people are joining the movement, some are also leaving. For those who remain in the Brahma Kumaris, the basic quality of their faith is strong, and their numbers continue to grow in spite of the strict standards required.

9

What About the Future?

Dadi Prakashmani died in 2007, but Dadi Janki is still alive although into her nineties. She is now supported by Dadi Gulzar and Dadi Ratan Mohini as co-administrative heads. They have received numerous honours yet have retained a simple lifestyle. Their lives have been exemplary. The Brahma Kumaris movement has celebrated its seventy-fifth anniversary and it is time to consider its future. Will it continue to be led by women? Will the 'transformation of the world as we now know it' come into being soon? Will celibacy continue to be important? And what, if anything, will be the relevance of the predominance of Indians in the university compared with people from other nations? Other matters are important, but these four topics appear to be crucial.

The Position of Women

Apart from the original male leadership by Dada Lekhraj, the Brahma Kumaris have been led by women. Dadi Janki and Dadi Gulzar are now advanced in years. Will they be succeeded by other women?

The high-profile of women in the Brahma Kumaris has been unique in religious terms because, unlike leaders of female orders such as nuns, their role has been to lead both men and women. Occasionally Hindu female saints such as Anandamayima have been recognised as such. Like Dadi Janki, Anandamayima was uneducated and untutored but her deep, child-like and spiritual simplicity and serenity were clear to all. Yet she was not the leader of an order of women or men. She was the spiritual centre of her own movement. She was *sui generis* (see Whaling, 2010, pp. 12–13).

The original reason for female leadership in the Brahma Kumaris arose from the situation in Sind, where women had been very much second-best and the time had come to redress the balance. In practice they have proved fine leaders during an era in which global female leadership has been somewhat scarce, although it has improved recently. During the confluence age women had the opportunity to show their mettle and successfully took it. There would therefore appear to be little reason to move away from female leadership, and the Brahma Kumaris may well continue with this tradition.

Millennial Markers

The answer to the second.question concerning the end of the world depends on what is meant by that term. The original visions of Brahma Baba had opened up the possibility of the transformation of the world as it is now, through some form of cataclysm, into a new golden age. At this point, there would be equality again between men and women until, in the final two ages, men would take over leadership again. Then during the next confluence age women would assume that role.

For many centuries some elements in many religious traditions have been forecasting the end of the world. At key times — for example, AD 500, 1000, 1500 and 2000 — such prophecies were made by various Christians but were not fulfilled. Even in-between times, on particular occasions, similar prophecies from various religions about the end of the world did not come to pass. When nothing happened, the religious tradition concerned adapted to the new situation. In *Expecting Armageddon: Essential Readings in Failed Prophecy*, Stone (2000) charts this process in regard to a number of traditions. As far as the Brahma Kumaris are concerned the possible millennial years of 1976 and 2008 (according to the Advance Party) have been and gone. Another possible key date will be 2036, the centenary of the beginning of the movement.

Jagdish Chander, in his many books, has identified symptoms of decline in the current world, and at the beginning of the nineteenth century Malthus forecasted bad times for the world. Undoubtedly, a number of things appear to be getting worse for the human race in recent years. Financial crises in Europe, the United States and elsewhere have had global implications, and severe famines have occurred in Somalia and the Horn of Africa. There have been tsunamis and floods in Asia, such as in Japan, which seriously affected atomic installations, and also in Pakistani Hyderabad, as well as potential changes to many environments through possible climate change and global warming. Meanwhile the threat of atomic escalation is virtually inevitable. Lying behind all this are deeper ecological matters. World population has reached seven billion, and is expected to reach nine billion in the next thirty years. Cities are growing and expanding throughout the world, and villages and small towns are declining. Water levels are falling so that wells have to go much deeper. More crops need to be grown. Forests are being cut down around the world. Species of animals are declining. In some places there is growing starvation. This 'litany of despair' could be extended. Problems seem to be deeper and more pressing than in the time of Malthus. It seems to be a not unreasonable time for the Brahma Kumaris to anticipate the end of the world as we know it now.

Different options lie open to the Brahma Kumaris World Spiritual University. Like the Advance Party it can hang on to a fundamentalist millenarian opinion that rejects any compromise with world-affirming views. For them the details of Brahma Baba's visions remain literally true through all ages and in all places. At the other extreme is a more world-affirming outlook as already described in respect of the work done by Brahma Kumaris in helping various people of various kinds to improve their self-confidence and human qualities, and in respect of work done with the United Nations, community help, and co-operation with scientific and other bodies.

The third option lies in the middle. It attempts to pay attention to both extremes with the aim of not ignoring the past and yet taking heed of the future. A factor affecting the third option relates to the advanced age of the present leaders, Dadi Janki and Dadi Gulzar. They represent, as it were, the Indian past of the movement and its beginning in Hyderabad, and also the present global ability of the university to innovate in complex fields that appear to be light-years away from where the Brahma Kumaris began. The person or persons who replace them as leaders may or may not be Indian, but they will inherit a movement that is still predominantly Indian numerically, and yet is present in more than a hundred nations. They will oversee a university that can help the world in the present in a spiritual and deep way, as well as one that will ponder the various possibilities of the future, including the end (or as they would call it the 'translation') of the world as we know it.

Celibacy

Another unique feature of the Brahma Kumaris is their stance against sexual intercourse. This occurred as a reaction to the predominance of men in the sexual realm, and their belief that women could enjoy lives of their own. However it is not purity in the sense of men and women working separately from one another, rather like monks and nuns. Brahma Kumars (men) and Brahma Kumaris (women) can and should be able to work together (and in the case of married Brahma Kumaris live together) but without sexual intercourse. It is clear that in the near future the stress on celibacy and purity will remain, even if there is no end to the world as we know it.

Indian Dominance

Currently eight Indian states — Maharashtra, Karnataka, Andhra Pradesh, Uttar Pradesh, Gujarat, Madhya Pradesh and Orissa — contain hundreds of Brahma Kumari centres, while each of the other states has slightly fewer centres than that. As far as cities are concerned, Delhi possesses more than a hundred centres. Bangalore, Mumbai, Ahmedabad and Hyderabad also have a substantial number. Other Indian cities have a growing set of centres. An increasing number of towns, and even some villages, also have centres. Even states on the periphery of, or just outside, India have their own centres — for example Assam, Himachal Pradesh, Jammu/Kashmir, Uttaranchal, Manipur, Arunachal Pradesh, Sikkim, Nagaland, Mizoram, Diu, Daman UT and Silvassa. In other words India and its environs have more than 7,500 centres, which are of deep importance to the whole movement and this clearly means that there are many more centres and many more members of the Brahma Kumaris in India than in the rest of the world put together. As numbers grow in India and in the rest of the world, how will this affect development of the university?

Its steady advance across the world has been helpful to Indians and non-Indians alike, in that it has opened up different insights for each another. It has also strengthened the sense of being part of a family of sisters and brothers with a worldwide presence. Now there is the spectacle of the Brahma Kumaris World Spiritual University becoming increasingly involved in altruistic activity on behalf of a world that was deemed to be beyond redemption. The spirituality that began in an isolated community of 400 people living a secluded life in Karachi has come to encompass the welfare of the world, a world whose end is supposedly nigh. We are in the realm of paradox. It is a paradox that is real but will doubtless find resolution in the thinking of the Brahma Kumaris. It will take time (if time allows) but there are signs that new thinking on this matter has already started.

Glossary

Amil — Hindu class of government servants

Artha — wealth or making a living; one of the four aims of life

avatars (*avatāras*) — incarnations of Vishnu

avyakt murlis — messages delivered through Dadi Gulzar

Bhagavad Gītā — very important text, part of *Mahābhārata*

Bhāgavata Purāna — important *Purāna* focusing on Krishna

bhakti — loving devotion, bhakti yoga, the way of loving devotion

bhog — special food

Brahma (Brahmā) — personal deity, part of trinity of Brahma, Vishnu and Shiva

brahmacharya (*brahmacārya*)— celibacy

Brahmin — the highest Hindu caste of priests

devi (*devī*) — goddess

dharma — moral order, righteousness, law, religion

drishti (*dṛṣṭi*) — gaze

Gītā Gyān — knowledge of Bhagavad *Gītā*

gopi (*gopī*) — milkmaid associated with Krishna

guru — teacher, spiritual master

Guru Granth Sahib — sacred Sikh text

gyan (*gyān*) — knowledge

jāti — sub-caste within the caste system

kali yuga (*kālī yuga*) — the iron age, the fourth, last and weakest of the four world ages

karma — works; action

Karmateet — not dependent on karma

Krishna (Kṛṣṇa) — avatāra of Vishnu; devotional deity in own right

Kshatriyas (Kṣatriyas) — the second Hindu caste of warriors and rulers

lingam (also *linga*)— phallic symbol of Shiva

Lohanas — Hindu community in Sind

Mahābhārata — Hindu Epic, longest epic in world history

moksha (*mokṣa*) — salvation; release from rebirth

mukhi — civic leader

murlis (murlīs) — messages for each day, akin to a kind of scripture

nakh — nail

nirvana (*nirvāṇa*) — liberation

panchayat — community assembly

pujari (*pūjāri*) – priest

ravan (*rāvaṇa*) — vice; demon king

sadhu (*sādhu*) — Hindu holy man or saint

sakar murlis — messages given by Brahma Baba when alive

sampradaya (sampradāya) — religious order or tradition

sannyasis (*saṃnyāsins*) — Hindu holy men

sanskars (*saṃskāras*) — impressions; innate tendencies; personality traits

satopradhan — pure

satsang — meeting

shakti (*śakti*) — power; goddess

Shankara (*Śaṅkara*) — Hindu philosopher

Shankaracharya (*Śaṅkarācārya*) — Hindu leader

shanti (*śānti*) — peace

Shiva (Śiva) — major deity

Shudras (Śūdras) — the fourth Hindu caste of servants

Swami (*Svāmī*) — lord

tapaswi — yogi

Udasis (Udāsīs) — people who worship the main Hindu gods

Vaishya (Vaiśya) — the third Hindu caste of artisans, traders

varna (*varṇa*) — general term for caste and the caste system

Veda — basic Hindu set of texts

Vishnu (Viṣṇu) — major deity, the Preserver, who sends forth avataras

yuga — age

References

BKWSU (1995) *A World in Transition*, Statement to UN World Summit for Social Development, London: Brahma Kumari Publications

BKWSU (n.d.) *Living, Learning, Loving*, Brochure of Brahma Kumaris World Spiritual University UK, London: Brahma Kumari Publications

Chander, J. (1983a) *A Brief Biography of Brahma Baba*, Mount Abu: Om Shanti Press, Brahma Kumaris World Spiritual University

Chander, J. (1983b) *Adi Dev: The First Man*, Mount Abu: Om Shanti Press, Brahma Kumaris World Spiritual University

Cobban, A. (1968) *Aspects of the French Revolution*, London: Cape

Eliot, T. S. (1944) 'Little Gidding', in *Four Quartets*, London: Faber & Faber

Green, M. (2008) *Article on Faith*, London: National Council for Voluntary Youth Services

Hodgkinson, Liz (2002) *Peace and Purity*, London: Ryder

Momen, W. with Momen, M. (2006) *Understanding the Baha'i Faith*, Edinburgh: Dunedin Academic Press

Om Rādhe, Brahma-kumārī (1943) *The Preordained Worldwide War of Mahabarata and its Result*, Karachi: Prajapati Brahma-Kumari Om Radhe

Panjabi, M. (Foreword) and Janki, Dadi (Afterward) (2008) *The Story of Immortality: A Return to Self-Sovereignty*, New York: Brahma Kumaris World Spiritual Organisation

Schweitzer, A. (1954) *The Quest of the Historical Jesus*, London: A. & C. Black

Stone, J. R. (ed.) (2000) *Expecting Armageddon: Essential Readings in Failed Prophecy*, London: Routledge

Walliss, J. (2002) *The Brahma Kumaris as a 'Reflexive Tradition'*, Aldershot; Burlington, NH: Ashgate

Weber, M. (1964) *The Sociology of Religion*, Boston: Beacon Press

Whaling, F. (1979) 'Sri Aurobindo: A critique', *Journal of Religious Studies*, Vol. VII, pp. 66–103

Whaling, F. (2010) *Understanding Hinduism*, Edinburgh: Dunedin Academic Press

Further Reading

Abbott, E. (2000) *A History of Celibacy*, London, New York, Sydney: Scribner

Babb, L. A. (1984) 'Indigenous feminism in a modern Hindu sect', *Signs: Journal of Women in Culture and Society*, Vol. 9, pp. 399–416

Babb, L. A. (1986) *Redemptive Encounters: Three Modern Styles in the Hindu Tradition*, London: University of California Press

Barg, R. (1992) *The Bhakti Sect of Vallabhacarya*, Delhi: Munshiram Manoharlal

Barratt, D. V. (1996) *Sects, Cults and Alternative Religions: A World Survey and Sourcebook*, London: Blandford

Bell, Christine (2006) *So Much Love*, London: Brahma Kumari Publications

Berg, J. (2006) *Touched by God*, London: Brahma Kumari Publications

Berger, P. (1967) *The Sacred Canopy*, New York: Doubleday

Bohm, David (1994) *Thought as a System*, London: Routledge

Carteret, Nikki de (2003) *Soul Power*, London: Brahma Kumari Publications

Chander, J. (1977) *The Way and the Goal of Raja Yoga*, Mount Abu: Om Shanti Press, Brahma Kumaris World Spiritual University

Chander, J. (1980) *Human Values, Moral Values and Spiritual Values*, Mount Abu: Om Shanti Press, Brahma Kumaris World Spiritual University

Chander, J. (1985) *The Eternal Drama of Souls, Matter and God*, Mount Abu: Om Shanti Press, Brahma Kumaris World Spiritual University

Chander, J. (1988a) *Science and Spirituality*, Mount Abu: Om Shanti Press, Brahma Kumaris World Spiritual University

Chander, J. (1988b) *The Eternal World Drama*, Mount Abu: Om Shanti Press, Brahma Kumaris World Spiritual University

Chander, J. (1996) *Visions of the Future*, Mount Abu: Om Shanti Press, Brahma Kumaris World Spiritual University

Chander, J. (2000) *Applied Spiritual Knowledge*, Mount Abu: Om Shanti Press, Brahma Kumaris World Spiritual University

Chander, J. (2001) *Building a Value-Based, Peaceful and Prosperous Society*, Mount Abu: Om Shanti Press, Brahma Kumaris World Spiritual University

Chander, J. (n.d.) *Brahma Baba — The Corporeal Medium of Shiva Baba*, Mount Abu: Om Shanti Press, Brahma Kumaris World Spiritual University

Chander, J. (n.d.) *Brahmacharya: Celibacy — The True Path to God Realisation*, Mount Abu: Om Shanti Press, Brahma Kumaris World Spiritual University

Chander, J. (n.d.) *Moral Values, Attitudes and Moods*, Mount Abu: Om Shanti Press, Brahma Kumaris World Spiritual University

Chander, J. (n.d.) *True Essence of Mahabharata and Gita*, Mount Abu: Om Shanti Press, Brahma Kumaris World Spiritual University

Cole, Dr Roger (1999) *Mission of Love: A Physician's Personal Journey Towards a Life Beyond*, London: Brahma Kumari Publications

Dawson, L. (1999) 'When prophecy fails and faith persists: A theoretical overview', *Nova Religio*, Vol. 3, No 1, pp. 60–82
Festinger, L., Riecken, H. W. and Schachter, S. (1964) *When Prophecy Fails*, New York: Harper Torchbook
George, M. (1999) *Discover Inner Peace*, London: Duncan Baird
George, M. (2004a) *1001 Meditations*, London: Brahma Kumari Publications
George, M. (2004b) *1001 Ways to Relax*, London: Brahma Kumari Publications
George, M. (2004c) *In the Light of Meditation*, London: Brahma Kumari Publications
Hodgkinson, Liz (1999) *Peace and Purity*, London: Ryder
Hodgkinson, Neville (ed.) (2008) *Melodies of Mama (Om Radhe)*, Mount Abu: Om Shanti Press
Howell, J. D. and Nelson, P. L. (1997), 'Structural adoption and "success" in the transplantation of an Asian new religious movement: The Brahma Kumaris in the western world', *Research in the Social Scientific Study of Religion*, Vol. 8, pp. 1–34
Janki, Dadi (1999a) *Pearls of Wisdom*, London: Brahma Kumari Publications
Janki, Dadi (1999b; 2nd edn) *Wings of Soul: The World and Wisdom of Dadi Janki*, London: Brahma Kumari Publications
Janki, Dadi (2003a) *Companion of God*, London: Brahma Kumari Publications
Janki, Dadi (2003b) *Inside Out: A Better Way of Living, Learning and Loving*, London: Brahma Kumari Publications
Janki, Dadi (2006) *A Pocket Book on Wisdom*, London: Brahma Kumari Publications
Janki, Dadi (2010) *Is There Another Way?*, New York: Sterling
Jayanti, B. K. (2000a) *Dreams and Reality*, London: Brahma Kumari Publications
Jayanti, B. K. (2000b) *The Art of Thinking*, London: Brahma Kumari Publications
Jayanti, B. K. (2006a) *A Pocket Book on Virtue*, London: Brahma Kumari Publications
Jayanti, B. K. (2006b) *God's Healing Power*, London: Brahma Kumari Publications
Jayanti, B. K. (2009a) *Practical Meditation*, London: Brahma Kumari Publications
Jayanti, B. K. (2009b; 2nd edn) *Spirituality in Daily Life*, London: Brahma Kumari Publications
King, Ursula (2009) *The Search for Spirituality*, Norwich: Canterbury Press
Malthus, T. R. (1798) *Essay on Population*, London: Macmillan
Mathur, L. S. (n.d.) *Raj Yoga as Experienced by a Scientist*, Mount Abu: Om Shanti Press
Melton, J. G. (2000) 'Spiritualisation and reformation: What really happens when prophecy fails', in Stone, J. R. (ed.) (2000) *Expecting Armageddon: Essential Readings in Failed Prophecy*, London: Routledge, pp. 145–57
Northey, Helen (ed.) (2010) *Mothers: The Spiritual Leaders (Spiritual Experiences of Brahma Kumari Mothers)*, Mount Abu: Om Shanti Press
O'Donnell, K. (2006; 7th edn) *New Beginnings, Raja Yoga Meditation Course*, London: Brahma Kumari Publications
O'Donnell, K. (2009) *Pathways to Higher Consciousness*, London: Brahma Kumari Publications
Panjabi, M. (Foreword) and Janki, Dadi (Afterward) (2008) *The Story of Immortality: A Return to Self-Sovereignty*, New York: Brahma Kumaris World Spiritual Organisation
Pemmel, J. (2003) *The Soul Illuminated*, London: Brahma Kumari Publications
Polatar, J. and Patel, M. (2009; 2nd edn) *Pure and Simple*, London: Brahma Kumari Publications
Prakash, A. (2010) *Bestower of Fortune (on Brahma Baba)*, Mount Abu: Om Shanti Press

Prakashmani, Dadi (ed.) (2002) *Pearls of Love from God (on Brahma Baba)*, Mount Abu: Om Shanti Press

Puttick, E. and Clarke, P. B. (eds) (1993) *Women as Teachers and Disciples in Traditional and New Religions*, New York: Edwin Mellon Press

Rodgers, J. and Naraine, G. (2009) *Something Beyond Greatness: Conversations with a Man of Science and a Woman of God*, London: Brahma Kumari Publications

Ryan, J. (2003) *In the Stillness: Meditations to Read*, London: Brahma Kumari Publications

Ryan, J. (2006) *Pathways to Happiness*, London: Brahma Kumari Publications

Skultans, V. (1993) 'The Brahma Kumaris and the role of women', in Puttick, E. and Clarke, P. B. (eds) (1993) *Women as Teachers and Disciples in Traditional and New Religions*, New York: Edwin Mellon Press, pp. 47–62

Stillerman, S. (ed.) (1998) *Wings of Soul: The Words and Wisdom of Dadi Janki*, London: Brahma Kumari Publications

Subirana, M. (2008a) *Dare to Live*, London: Brahma Kumari Publications

Subirana, M. (2008b) *Who Rules in Your Life?*, London: Brahma Kumari Publications

Thakur, U. T. (1959) *Sindhi Culture*, Bombay: University of Bombay Press

Trano, A (1999; 2nd edn), *The Alpha Point*, London: Brahma Kumari Publications

Trano, A. (2003) *Reflections: for Dawn, Day and Dusk*, London: Brahma Kumari Publications

Trano, A. (2006) *Eastern Thought for the Western Mind*, London: Brahma Kumari Publications

Trano, A. (2011) *Remember: A Journey Back to the Essence*, London: Brahma Kumari Publications

Walliss, J. (1999) 'From world rejection to ambivalence: The development of millenarianism in the Brahma Kumaris', *Journal of Contemporary Religion*, Vol. 14, No. 3, pp. 375–85

Ward, C. T. (2008) *The Four Faces of Women*, London: Brahma Kumari Publications

Whaling, F. (1995) 'The Brahma Kumaris', *Journal of Contemporary Religion*, Vol. 10, No. 1, pp. 3–28

Index

Glossary entries are in **bold**. Page numbers in *italics* denote illustrations